THE MASS
OLD FORT MACKINAC
{ *MICHILIMACKINAC* }

A TRAGEDY OF THE AMERICAN FRONTIER

With the Early History of St. Ignace, Mackinaw City and Mackinac Island

CONTAINING: *An Explanation of the Meaning of the Name Mackinac—A Brief History of the Straits Region, Including an Account of Father Marquette's Mission; LaSalle and Cadillac at St. Ignace—The Marquette-Jolliet Voyage to the Mississippi River—A Description of Early American Frontier Life—The Fur Traders—Birch-Bark Canoes—Major Robert Rogers at Michilimackinac—The Mormon Kingdom of Michigan—John Jacob Astor's American Fur Company—Dr. Beaumont's Discoveries in Digestion—Facts about the Famous Chief Pontiac and His Indian War—Details about the Indian Ball Game Used as a Blind for the Attack upon Fort Michilimackinac—The Massacre of the English—Adventures and Escapes of the English Fur Trader, Alexander Henry—Various Details about Indian Life and Character.*

By RAYMOND MCCOY

With Many Illustrations and Maps

NOTES

On page 13 reference is made to automobile ferries. When the Mackinac Bridge was opened in November, 1957, the operation of these ferries was discontinued.

On page 54 the hope is expressed that Fort Michilimackinac might someday be restored. This hope has been realized through the efforts of the Mackinac Island State Park Commission.

On page 63 the old retail store of the American Fur Co. is identified as the Early Cottage at the base of the fort hill. This building is now the Beaumont Memorial Building, restored in July, 1954, by the Michigan State Medical Society, aided by Parke, Davis & Co.

Published By

Raymond McCoy

1409 N. Lincoln St.

Bay City, Michigan

Eighth Edition

PREFACE

THE purpose of this little book is to present, in a popular way, something of the interesting story that is associated with one of the most historic regions on the North American continent—the region around the Straits of Mackinac, in Michigan.

Although it has been printed in an inexpensive form, a serious effort has been exerted to make the work thoroughly accurate; and I believe that it will be found to possess something of value for almost everyone interested in the early pioneer phase of American history.

The first chapter of the pages which follow, contains a short general history of the Mackinac country; while the rest of the book is devoted to a detailed account of what impresses me as the most dramatic happening in the eventful history of the region—that is, the massacre of the British inhabitants of Old Fort Michilimackinac, in June, 1763.

Because of their patience in answering my many inquiries about doubtful matters relating to the subject, I am indebted to: Dr. Milo M. Quaife, of the Burton Historical Library; Dr. George N. Fuller, of the Michigan Historical Commission; Dr. W. B. Hinsdale and Dr. E. F. Greenman, of the University of Michigan; Dr. Randolph G. Adams and Mr. Howard Peckham, of the W. L. Clements Library; Dr. Louise Phelps Kellogg, of the Wisconsin State Historical Society; Dr. L. H. Shattuck of the Chicago Historical Society; Father Gilber J. Garraghan and Father Jean Delanglez, o. Loyola University, Chicago; Miss Grace Lee Nute of the Minnesota Historical Society; Mr. Robert W. Bingham, of the Buffalo Historical Society; Professor Allan Nevins, of Columbia University; Dr.

James F. Kenney, of the Public Archives of Canada, and to the late Father William F. Gagnieur, of Sault Ste. Marie. Most of those named have also been helpful in suggesting changes which they considered desirable in the previous printings of the book, in order to make it as reliable as possible. Dr. Quaife has been especially kind in consenting to read the manuscript and in offering valuable suggestions for its improvement. However, while I have received the aid of historians and scientists, the responsibility for what appears in these pages is mine alone.

I am also indebted for the use of the facilities of the Bay City Public Library; the Burton Historical Library, Detroit; the W. L. Clements Library, Ann Arbor; and the Ayer Collection of the Newberry Library, Chicago. My obligation to the authors of the books included in the reading list at the end of this narrative will be obvious to anyone familiar with these works. It was from them that I obtained much of my material.

—R. Mc.

Bay City, Mich.
June, 1956

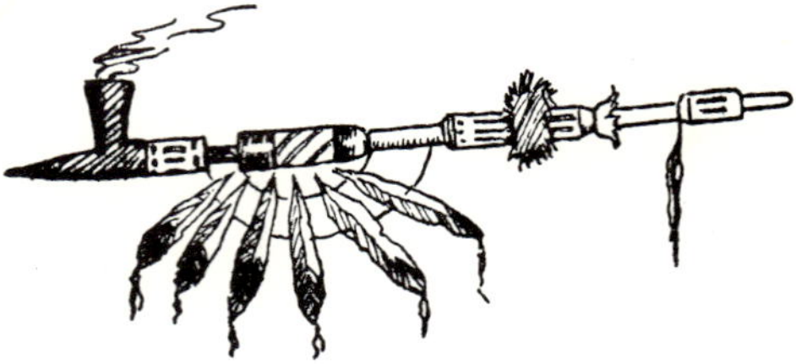

"As our Country grows and its population increases—as it will—care must be taken to have each succeeding generation know the trials and tribulations of those who preceded them. History is an essential study to better government."—**George Washington.**

MEANING OF THE NAME MACKINAC

THE name Mackinac comes from the Indians. It is derived from Michilimackinac, the name by which the Straits Region was known among Indians and early white men for many years. Its meaning has been explained in a variety of ways, but the familiar translation of "Great Turtle" (which some say is suggested by the shape of Mackinac Island) possesses the advantage of a longer and more general usage.

Reports of the early Jesuit missionaries tell us that this was the name of a tribe of Indians, the Michilimackinacs, who once made their home on Mackinac Island. Their totem, or clan emblem, was the turtle. During the numerous wars fought between the Iroquois tribes of New York, and the Indians of the Great Lakes region, the Michilimackinacs were exterminated; and, according to an Indian tradition, the Ottawa and Ojibwa (or Chippewa) Indians named the Island after their departed friends and neighbors.

Starting with the Island, the name in time came to designate the Straits Region generally—including the present sites of St. Ignace and Mackinaw City. The term Michilimackinac is no longer used, and the Island and Straits are now called simply Mackinac, with the French ending "ac." This is pronounced MACK-INAW, (rhyming with "law") the same as the name of Mackinaw City, on the tip of Michigan's lower peninsula. The name of this latter community is spelled the same as it is pronounced in order to distinguish the locality from Mackinac Island.

AN INTRODUCTORY HISTORY OF

MACKINAC AND ST. IGNACE

Father Marquette's Mission

MANY years before most of the numerous present-day cities, towns and villages west of the Allegheny Mountains were established, white men had, at various times, built three fortified settlements along the shores of the Straits of Mackinac—the first at St. Ignace, the second at Mackinaw City and the third at Mackinac Island. All three places were known by the name of Michilimackinac, or Mackinac.

The first of these settlements was located on the northern side of the Straits where the city of St. Ignace now stands. It was founded in the summer of 1671 by Father Jacques Marquette, a 34-year-old French Jesuit missionary, who built an Indian mission on the site—"a rude and unshapely chapel, its sides of logs and its roof of bark."

Father Marquette was a native of the ancient, battle-scarred city of Laon, in northeastern France. His Canadian superior describes him as "robust of body"; and, by temperament, he was gentle, retiring and deeply religious. He lived at a time when an intense religious revival was taking place in France, then the greatest Roman Catholic country in the world. One of the purposes of this revival was to build up the Church among the Indians of North America, where the French had planted a colony along the banks of the St. Lawrence River in and around Quebec (founded by Samuel de Champlain in 1608) and Montreal. The national heroes of France, in those days, were religious martyrs; and the highest ambition of a large number of the French,

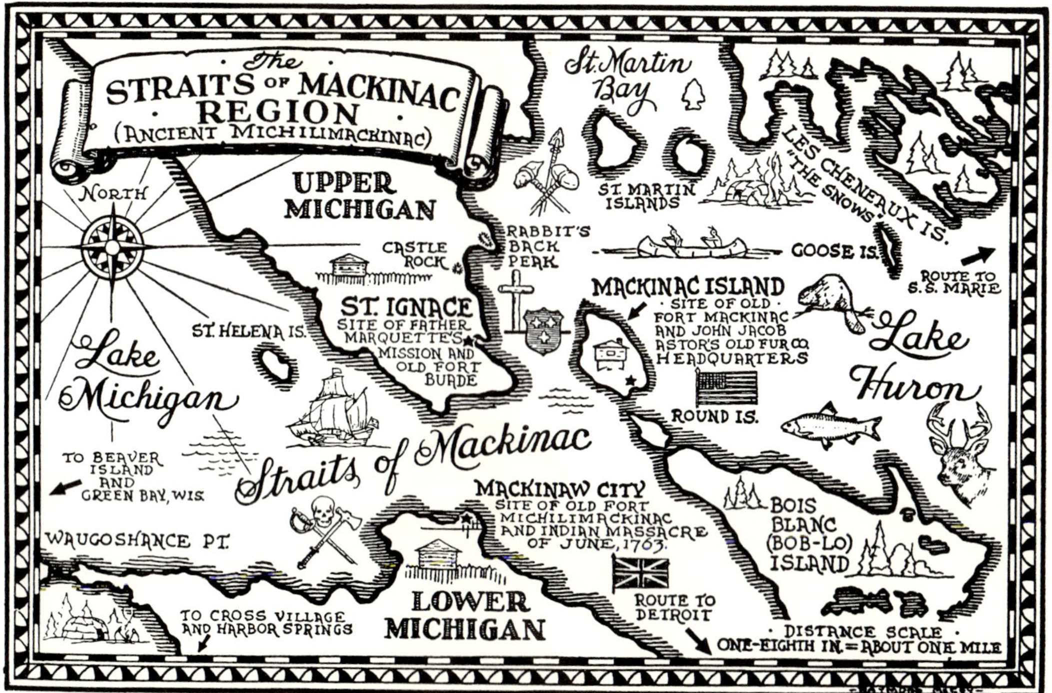
The STRAITS OF MACKINAC REGION
(ANCIENT MICHILIMACKINAC)
NORTH
UPPER MICHIGAN
CASTLE ROCK
ST. IGNACE
SITE OF FATHER MARQUETTE'S MISSION AND OLD FORT BUADE
ST. HELENA IS.
Lake Michigan
TO BEAVER ISLAND AND GREEN BAY, WIS.
Straits of Mackinac
WAUGOSHANCE PT.
TO CROSS VILLAGE AND HARBOR SPRINGS
LOWER MICHIGAN
MACKINAW CITY
SITE OF OLD FORT MICHILIMACKINAC AND INDIAN MASSACRE OF JUNE, 1763.
ROUTE TO DETROIT
St. Martin Bay
ST. MARTIN ISLANDS
RABBIT'S BACK PEAK
MACKINAC ISLAND
· SITE OF OLD · FORT MACKINAC AND JOHN JACOB ASTOR'S OLD FUR CO. HEADQUARTERS
ROUND IS.
GOOSE IS.
LES CHENEAUX IS.
"THE SNOWS"
ROUTE TO S. S. MARIE
Lake Huron
BOIS BLANC (BOB-LO) ISLAND
· DISTANCE SCALE ·
ONE-EIGHTH IN. = ABOUT ONE MILE

and other people of Europe, was to suffer and die for Christianity, and in this way to win a certain passport to heaven. Like many another young missionary, Father Marquette became inspired by this holy zeal. He left a comfortable home in a civilized society to cross the ocean to a distant wilderness and face all sorts of suffering, hardship and death, among a savage people, in order to win converts to the Christian religion. Although he had been in America only five years, Marquette had already mastered six Indian dialects; he had aided in beginning a mission at Sault Ste. Marie, in 1668,—the first center of white activity in Michigan—and he had served for a time at the mission of La Pointe de St. Esprit, on Lake Superior, near the present Ashland, Wis. From the latter place he and his savage flock had fled to Michilimackinac before a threatened attack by the Sioux (or Dakota) Indians. A number of years before, the Huron and Ottawa Indians,—among whom Marquette had his mission—had made their home at Michilimackinac, but about 1650 they were driven westward by the warlike Iroquois tribes, of New York. And while they still feared the Iroquois, for the time being they feared the Sioux more, particularly since they had heard that a period of peace with the Iroquois was then in prospect.

Arrival of Fur Traders

At Michilimackinac, Marquette called his new wilderness church the Mission of St. Ignace, after St. Ignatius Loyola, the founder of the Jesuit order of the priesthood. And as time went on, a small community sprang up nearby as French fur traders came to trade with the neighboring Huron and Ottawa tribes, and erected their log dwellings along the waterfront. These traders were in quest of the skins of various fur-bearing animals—beavers, otters, minks, muskrats, etc.—which were

Drawing made from an oil painting discovered in Montreal in 1897, which is alleged to be a portrait of Father Jacques Marquette, who began an Indian mission at Michilimackinac in 1671, on the present site of St. Ignace, Mich. In 1668 Marquette founded a mission at Sault Ste. Marie which was the first known building erected by white men in the State of Michigan. In 1673 he and Louis Jolliet discovered the upper Mississippi River at Prairie du Chien, Wis. and explored its course, in birch-bark canoes, as far South as the mouth of the Arkansas River. The autograph above, written in Latin, is from the religious vows taken by Father Marquette at Sault Ste. Marie in July, 1671.

obtained from the Indians in exchange for such articles as blankets, knives, kettles, muskets, axes, ornaments, etc. The furs thus obtained were shipped to France, where they were made into clothing for the wealthy people of Europe; while the money paid for the furs served as the chief income of the French inhabitants of Canada. When the French first came to America, it was the custom of the Indians to carry their animal skins to Montreal each spring, for trading during the big fur fair which was held at that time. But gradually, young Frenchmen began to follow the Indians into the interior regions in order to obtain more and more furs; and the traders who took up quarters at Michilimackinac, near Marquette's mission, had doubtless come in this way.

Importance of Mackinac

The settlement thus begun, and the two others at Michilimackinac which succeeded it, were among the earliest beginnings of civilization in the region northwest of the Ohio River, once known as the Northwest Territory. Each of the three settlements served as a gathering place, or base of operations, for the throng of hardy pioneers who opened the way to the vast country which now forms the states of Ohio, Indiana, Illinois, Wisconsin, Michigan, and a part of Minnesota. For, located as it was, in the heart of some of the best fur-trading country, at the junction of Lakes Huron, Michigan and Superior, and with early transportation almost entirely by water, Michilimackinac was a natural stopping-off place for early travelers. It lay midway along the route between the East and the waterways of the Mississippi and, like ancient Rome, all roads led to it.

Trentanove's stalue of Father ɪɪarquette (it is not an attempt at a portrait) in Statuary Hall of the National Capitol, in Washington—a tribute from the State of Wisconsin. A replica of this statue is to be seen on Mackinac Island and in Marquette, Mich.

French Claim Upper Lakes Region

About the time that Father Marquette was beginning his mission of St. Ignace (it appears that he was then still at the mission of St. Esprit), the French held a picturesque ceremony at Sault Ste. Marie, to take formal possession of the upper Great Lakes region, of which the site of Marquette's mission was a part. On the morning of June 14, 1671, a mixed concourse assembled on a spot overlooking the rapids of the St. Mary's River. It was composed of black-robed Jesuit missionaries; Indian chiefs in their best savage dress, summoned from far and near for the occasion; and French soldiers and fur traders.

A large cross, and a cedar post bearing a metal plate with the arms of France, were planted side by side in the ground; and Duamont de St. Lusson, agent of the governor of Canada, dressed in the colorful uniform of a French officer of the seventeenth century, stepped forward. Holding his sword in one hand, and raising a sod of earth with the other, he proclaimed in a loud voice: "In the name of the Most High, Most Mighty and Most Redoubted Monarch, Louis, Fourteenth of that name, Most Christian King of France and of Navarre, I take possession of this place, Sainte Marie du Sault, as also of Lakes Huron and Superior, the Island of Caientonon (Manitoulin), and all countries, rivers, lakes and streams contiguous and adjacent thereunto; both those which have been discovered and those which may be discovered hereafter, in all their length and breadth, bounded on the one side by the seas of the North and of the West, and on the other by the South Sea; declaring to the nations thereof that from this time forth they are dependent on his Majesty, bound to obey his laws and follow his customs; promising them on his part all succor and protec-

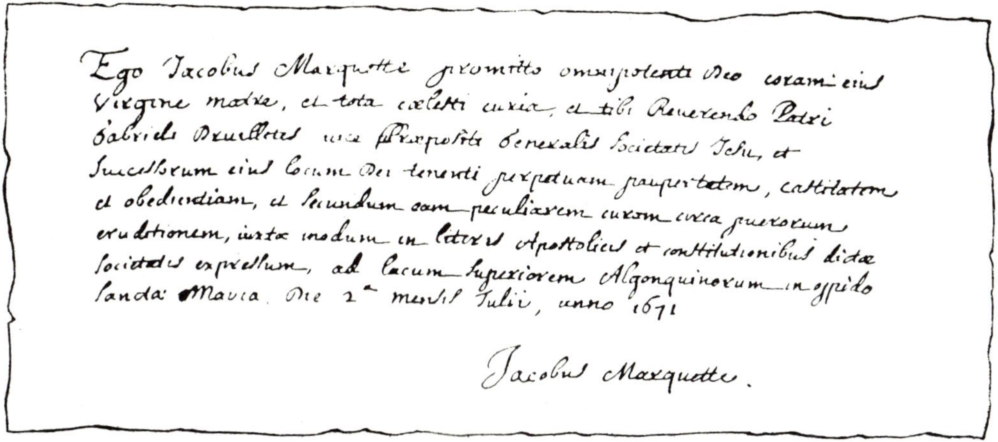
Ego Jacobus Marquette promitto omnipotenti Deo coram eius
Virgine matre, et tota caelesti curia, et tibi Reverendo Patri
Gabrieli Druillettes vice Praepositi Generalis Societatis Jesu, et
Successorum eius locum Dei tenenti perpetuam paupertatem, castitatem
et obedientiam, et secundum eam peculiarem curam circa puerorum
eruditionem, iuxta modum in litteris Apostolicis et constitutionibus dictae
Societatis expressum, ad Lacum Superiorem Algonquinorum in oppido
Sanctae Mariae Die 2a mensis Julii, anno 1671

Jacobus Marquette.

This is a specimen of Father Marquette's handwriting. The document is the "last" or "final" vows taken by Marquette as a Jesuit priest, while he was at Sault Ste. Marie, in 1671. It is written in Latin and a translation of it reads: "I, Jacques Marquette, promise to Almighty God, in the presence of His Virgin Mother and the whole heavenly court, and to you Reverend Father Gabriel Druilletes, in place of the General of the Society of Jesus and his successors, God's vice-gerents, perpetual poverty, chastity and obedience, and, conformably to obedience, special care for the instruction of youth in the manner expressed in the Apostolic letters and constitutions of the said Society. At Lake Superior of the Algonquins in the town of St. Mary's, the 2nd day of July, 1671. Jacques Marquette." The original manuscript is in the Jesuit General Archives, in Rome, Italy.

tion against the incursions and invasions of their enemies; declaring to all other potentates, princes, sovereigns, states and republics,—to them and their subjects—that they cannot and are not to seize or settle upon any parts of the aforesaid countries, save only under the good pleasure of His Most Christian Majesty, and of him who will govern in his behalf; and this on pain of incurring his resentment and the effects of his arms. Vive le Roi."

The Frenchmen then fired a volley of musketry and shouted "Vive le Roi" (Long live the King), while the Indians stood wondering about the meaning of it all. Thus by means of a few sentences, uttered by a feeble human voice—which probably could not be heard at more than a few hundred yards—a vast region, embracing thousands of square miles, was claimed as a possession of a foreign ruler living over four thousand miles away.

Marquette and Jolliet Voyage to Mississippi

After establishing his mission, Father Marquette remained among the Indians and roving fur traders at Michilimackinac for about two years, baptizing the young and old and giving instructions in the Roman Catholic religion. For the most part, the savages appear to have received his teachings with indifference; but, undaunted, Marquette wrote to his superior: "We must have patience with untutored minds who know only the devil, who like their ancestors, have been his slaves, and who often relapse into the sins in which they were nurtured. God alone can fix these fickle minds and place and keep them in His grace and touch their hearts while we stammer in their ears."

The interior parts of the North American continent were largely unknown among white men in those days, and much speculating went on among the French concerning a "great river" which they often heard the Indians tell about. The French were interested in knowing whether this "great river"—the Mississippi—provided a cross-country passage to the Orient, for this was an object much sought after at that time. With the distance across North America and the Pacific Ocean still unknown, it was hoped that such a passage would prove to be a less difficult way than the old eastern caravan routes of reaching China, India and the Spice Islands; from where the people of Europe obtained spices, silks, incense and precious stones. (It will be recalled that Columbus was looking for a western water route to the Orient when he discovered America.) Spices, in particular, were then in great demand because in those early times, before the introduction of cold storage, food spoiled quickly, and it tasted much better after it had been seasoned freely with pepper, nutmeg, clove, ginger, etc.

So, after about two years of missionary labors among the backsliding tribesmen at the first settlement at Michilimackinac, Father Marquette was assigned, along with Louis Jolliet, a trader and explorer, to locate this "great river" and find out where it flowed. Together, at Michilimackinac, with the aid of the local Indians, the two men planned their famous voyage; and in May, 1673, they set out from here in two birch-bark canoes, with five men and a supply of dried meat and Indian corn, to make their important discovery. Crossing Lake Michigan, and what is now Wisconsin, they entered the Mississippi River, about a month later (June 17th), at the site of the present Prairie du Chien, with a feeling which Marquette describes as "a joy which I cannot express." Steering their canoes southward on the

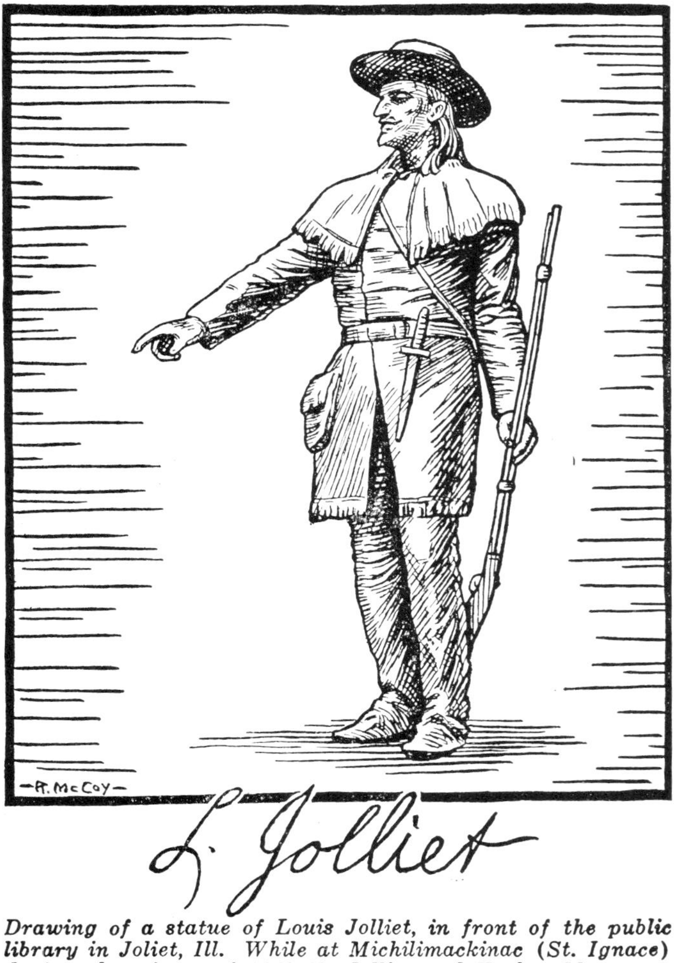

Drawing of a statue of Louis Jolliet, in front of the public library in Joliet, Ill. While at Michilimackinac (St. Ignace) during the winter of 1672-73, Jolliet and Father Marquette planned their famous journey to the Mississippi River. And in May, 1673, they set out from this site of Marquette's mission on their voyage of discovery and exploration. The autograph above is from Justin Winsor's "Narrative and Critical History of America."

broad swirling waters of the river, the Frenchmen continued downstream amid a panorama of scattered Indian villages; limitless stretches of prairie lands; and herds of grazing buffaloes, which stared stupidly through tangled manes at the strangers.

At length, upon reaching the mouth of the Arkansas River, the explorers became convinced that they had gone far enough to prove that the Mississippi ran into the Gulf of Mexico, and not into the Gulf of California, or the Atlantic Ocean, —and since they feared being captured by the Spaniards—they started back homeward. Upon their return, Marquette stopped off at the mission near Green Bay, Wis., to recover from an attack of dysentery, and to write his account of the expedition; while Jolliet continued on to Quebec with his report to the governor. Good luck had favored the travelers throughout the long and dangerous voyage; but now, as Jolliet drew near home—after passing forty-two rapids, and when all danger seemed past—fortune deserted him. A short distance from Montreal, his canoe was upset in the Lachine Rapids; his companions were drowned, and all his notes and maps concerning the trip to the Mississippi, were lost. In this way, it happened that, in depending almost solely on Father Marquette's report for the story of the discoveries that had been made—along with the fact that he was a Jesuit missionary and his fellow-Jesuits emphasized his part in the expedition—this self-effacing priest was raised, by 19th Century writers, to the position of the sole hero of the voyage. That is why Father Marquette's name is more commonly associated with the discovery of the Mississippi River than that of his fellow-traveler, Louis Jolliet, who, as the official agent of the government, was the leader of the undertaking.

Marquette Buried at St. Ignace

While journeying across Illinois, Father Marquette had promised the Illinois Indians that he would return and establish a mission among them. And it was while he was on his way back to St. Ignace, after a second voyage to the Illinois tribes, during which he preached to these Indians, that he died of dysentery, along the eastern shore of Lake Michigan, near the present site of Ludington. This was in the spring of 1675. Two years later, a party of Indians, whom Marquette had once instructed, dug up his body; carefully dissected and cleaned the bones, after a racial custom of theirs; put them in a birch-bark coffin and bore them to Michilimackinac. Here, following a solemn ceremony, Father Marquette's remains were buried beneath the floor of his Mission of St. Ignace.

LaSalle Visits St. Ignace in the "Griffin"

Two years after Marquette's funeral, the little bay at St. Ignace—where automobile and railway ferries now regularly come and go—was visited by the "Griffin," the first sailing vessel to appear on the upper Great Lakes. This was in August, 1679, when Robert Cavelier de La Salle, the famous French explorer, paused at Michilimackinac for about a week, on his voyage in the "Griffin," from Niagara Falls (LaSalle), N. Y., to Green Bay, Wis. Dressed in a scarlet cloak with gold lace, La Salle went ashore with his men to visit the Huron and Ottawa Indians and to celebrate mass in the Ottawa village. Meanwhile, the Indians paddled their frail canoes about the "Griffin," struck with wonder at the sight of this strange, but "fine wooden canoe," as they called it. To add to their astonishment, the Frenchmen fired the ship's cannon, and the deafening roar completely bewildered the tribesmen, who had never experienced anything of the sort before.

Drawing of Gudebrod's statue of Robert Cavelier de La Salle, the famous French explorer, who stopped at Michilimackinac (then at St. Ignace) in August, 1679, during his voyage in the "Griffin," the first sailing ship on the upper Great Lakes. La Salle also visited St. Ignace on two other occasions while traveling between Montreal and his fort on the Illinois River. The autograph is from the Chicago Historical Society.

An Early Glimpse of Detroit

As La Salle and his followers approached Michilimackinac on the trip up through the strait (in French, *detroit*), now called the Detroit River, the Frenchmen saw what impressed them as a real paradise on earth. This was in August, 1679, —twenty-two years before Cadillac founded Detroit—and nature everywhere lay untouched by the hands of white men. On both sides of the river there were green prairies bordered by lofty trees, from which vines of luscious grapes were hanging; and bears, deer, swans and wild turkeys were seen in abundance. Father Louis Hennepin, the Franciscan journalist of the expedition, was thoroughly fascinated by the scene, and he wrote: "Those who will one day have the happiness to possess this fertile and pleasant strait will be very much obliged to those who have shown them the way."

Crossing Lake St. Clair—which they named after the day on which they traversed its shallow waters—and passing up the St. Clair River, the travelers soon entered the broad, uncharted expanse of Lake Huron. Here the "Griffin" ran into a fierce squall which seemed to foretell the ship's early destruction. The little 45-ton vessel pitched and tossed alarmingly, and terror reigned among everyone on board. Even the brave La Salle was overcome by fear, and he called on his men to prepare for the worst. All kneeled in prayer and clamored to the saints, straining to make themselves heard above the wind howling through the rigging. All, that is, except Lucas, the godless pilot, who, with every resource of a veteran salt-water sailor, occupied himself with loudly cursing and swearing at La Salle. More concerned about his honor than about his life, he was in a fury with La Salle for bringing him to die—as he

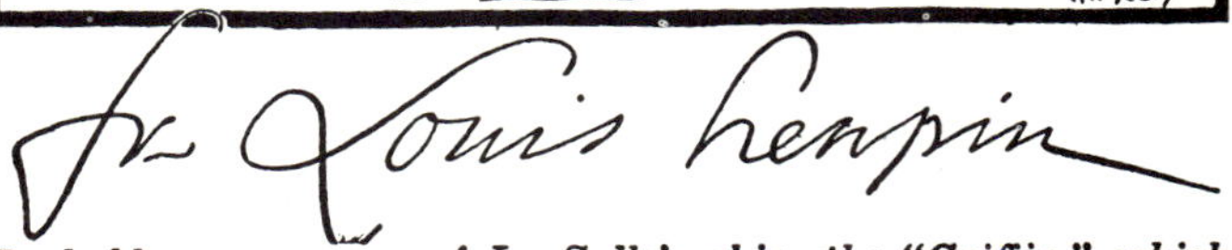

Probable appearance of La Salle's ship, the "Griffin," which stopped at Michilimackinac (St. Ignace) for about a week, in the late summer of 1679. This was the first vessel larger than a canoe to appear on the Great Lakes west of the Niagara River; and it was thus the trail-blazer for the vast fleet of freighters and passenger boats which sail the upper Great Lakes today. This drawing is based on the ship designs of the 17th Century, and on the description of Father Louis Hennepin, a fellow-traveler of La Salle on the "Griffin." The autograph is from one of Hennepin's letters in the Bibliotheque Nationale, in Paris.

regarded it—disgracefully, in a "dirty lake" of fresh water, after his long and honorable career of sailing the ocean. At length, the Frenchmen's prayers were heard; the angry winds abated, and the vessel reached Michilimackinac in safety. From here the "Griffin" set sail for Green Bay, where La Salle loaded the ship with a cargo of furs and sent it back to Niagara, in charge of the pilot. Nothing was ever heard of the "Griffin" after this. And to the present day, despite occasional reports of the finding of her wreckage, nobody knows whether this pioneer of Great Lakes ships —the forerunner of the large steamers and freighters which sail the upper lakes today—was swallowed up in a storm, burned by Indians or made the prize of a crew of traitors.

War and Indian Diplomacy

During these early years when the first settlement at Michilimackinac was being established, the French and the Iroquois Indians, of New York, were frequently at war, or on the verge of going to war. In these struggles the French were usually aided by their Indian allies, the Huron and Ottawa tribes of Michilimackinac, and other Indians from the Great Lakes region. These Indians were recruited and led eastward to the scene of battle by M. de La Durantaye and M. Louvigny, commandants at Michilimackinac; and Nicolas Perrot, a noted wood-ranger and Indian expert.

Growing weary of this endless warfare, the governor of Canada, Denonville, in 1688, decided to try his hand at bringing about peace by negotiation. He succeeded in getting the Iroquois to agree to a treaty of peace, but it was a treaty which would leave the Iroquois free to continue the war against the Great Lakes Indians, who would thus be unaided. While these peace talks

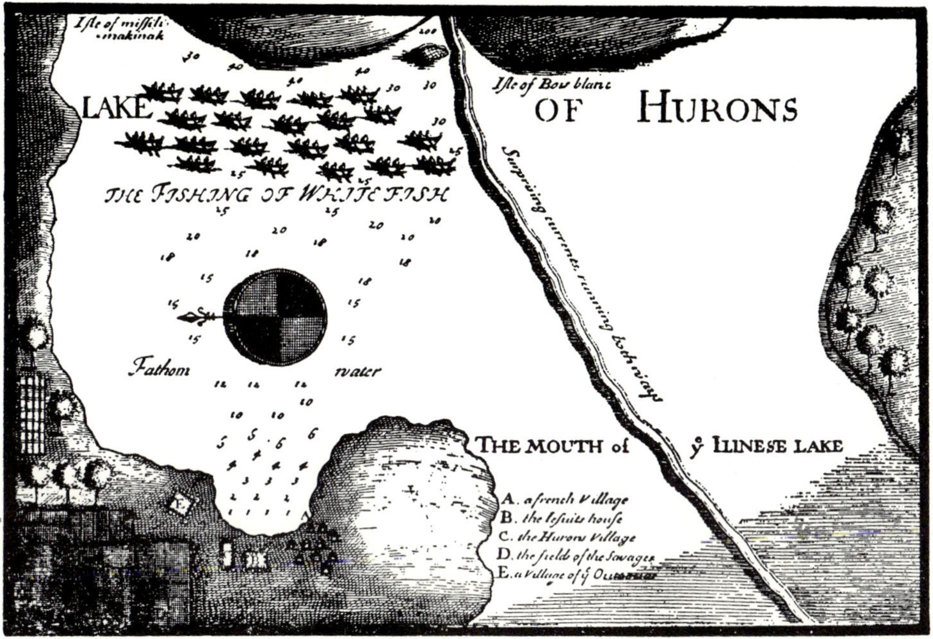

Baron La Hontan's map of Michilimakinac (St. Ignace), in the year 1688, which indicates that the settlement at Michilimackinac did not include a fort at that time.

were going on, Kondiaronk, or The Rat, a distinguished Huron chieftain, of Michilimackinac, whose high intelligence is attested to by early travelers, got together a party of warriors and journeyed eastward in quest of Iroquois scalps. Upon arriving at Fort Frontenac (now Kingston, Ontario), he was informed of the separate peace, and told he had better return to Michilimackinac, as messengers were expected soon from the Iroquois to conclude the treaty. Although he pretended to be unconcerned by this news, The Rat was amazed at this betrayal of his people by the French; for the French had promised to continue the war until the Iroquois were destroyed; yet, now they were arranging to desert their Indian allies, leaving them to bear the full force of an Iroquois attack without help.

What followed was a bit of political scheming which would have done credit to even so great a diplomat as the wily Cardinal Richelieu, a former prime minister of France. The Rat had secretly learned the route of the expected deputies, and he paddled off, not as he pretended, for Michilimackinac, but for the place where he knew he could intercept the Iroquois peace messengers. Arriving at a point along the southeastern shore of Lake Ontario (near the present Pulaski, N. Y.), The Rat and his men hid in ambush; and a few days later when the Iroquois delegates passed, they showered them with a volley of bullets, killing one chief and wounding all the rest of the party. They then rushed upon the Iroquois and bound them as prisoners; the victims meanwhile protesting that they were envoys of peace. Upon hearing this, The Rat explained that he was merely acting on orders from the French governor, and he professed to be amazed and horrified at the French for using him for so dark a purpose. He then released the Iroquois, cursed the French governor, and said that "Though there is war between us, I give you your liberty." He added that since the governor of Canada had made him take part in such a dishonorable act he would never be happy until the Iroquois had taken "a just vengeance upon him." Then returning to Fort Frontenac he said cooly, "I have killed the peace; we shall see how the governor will get out of this business."

Making his way home to Michilimackinac with an Iroquois prisoner whom he had kept, as was customary among Indians, to replace one of his men that had been killed in the skirmish, The Rat turned him over to the commandant who had not learned, at his distant post, of the peace negotiations. The Iroquois protested that he was on an errand of peace when captured, but The Rat insisted that he was crazy; whereupon the captive was shot by a file of soldiers. To complete his design, The Rat then took an old Iroquois, who had been a prisoner at St. Ignace for some time, and told him he was free to return to his people and tell them of the cruelty of the French, who had put his fellow tribesman to death. The released prisoner faithfully carried out this mission; and the fruit of all this Indian diplomacy was an Iroquois attack, in August, 1689, upon the French village of Lachine (near Montreal), which has been described as the "most frightful massacre in Canadian history." Houses were burned and men, women and children were butchered without discrimination. And as the Iroquois passed the French forts, upon leaving the scene of destruction and death, they shouted to the soldiers, "You deceived us, and now we have deceived you." By such means the French peace efforts were ruined—and the military alliance between the French and the Great Lakes Indians against the Iroquois was preserved.

Fort Constructed at St. Ignace

With the increase in size and importance of the settlement at Michilimackinac, the French sent a detachment of trained soldiers, and a stockade, or log fort, was built. This post appears to have been erected some time between August, 1688, and July, 1689. Although no fort is shown on Baron La Hontan's Michilimackinac map of 1688, a fort of some kind had been built by July 25, 1689, since on that date LaDurantaye, the commandant, sent in his bill of expenses for erecting a "reduit," or place of shelter, which had been authorized by the King of France in March, 1688.

But whatever the date of its construction, the stronghold, according to a map of about 1717, was located along the shore of the bay, southeast of Father Marquette's mission—about where the business section of St. Ignace now stands.

Cadillac at St. Ignace

In 1694, this fort,—no doubt then much enlarged—and the adjoining settlement, were in charge of Captain Antoine de Lamothe-Cadillac, who served as commandant, or military governor. Cadillac describes the place then as "one of the largest in all Canada" (what is now Michigan was then a part of Canada), and as "the rendezvous of the chiefs of all the nations in the surrounding country." It consisted of "a fine fort of pickets," which Cadillac called Fort Buade, after the family name of Louis de Buade, Count of Palluau and Frontenac, the ablest of the French governors of Canada. The post was garrisoned by trained soldiers; while the log houses of the traders were said to be about sixty in number. The Indian inhabitants had increased to several thousand, and their corn fields, which provided corn for both the French and Indians, extend-

*An imaginative picture of Captain **Antoine de Lamothe-Cadillac**, commandant of Michilimackinac (St. Ignace), 1694-97, and founder of the city of Detroit, in **July**, 1701. This drawing **is** based on the general appearance of **French** infantry officers of Cadillac's time. The autograph **is from** an original Cadillac letter in the Burton Historical Collection, Detroit.*

ed among the charred stumps and fallen trees for a considerable distance around the settlement. These fields, as was customary among the Indians, were attended by the squaws; because with the female controlling reproduction, the Indians reasoned that the crops would be better if planted and cared for by women. The corn from these fields the tribesmen placed in a log, hollowed out by burnings and scrapings (a mortar), and pounded it into a kind of hominy. This, when boiled in water and flavored with fish, meat or fats, was rated a favorite dish. It was called *sagamite*, and appears to have been quite common among Indians all over the country.

The Bootleg Fur Traders

As for the general aspect of the settlement, the place had drifted a long way from its pious beginning as the site of Father Marquette's mission, and it was now the favorite haunt of the *coureurs de bois* (the wood-rangers, or unlicensed fur traders); and squaws and brandy abounded. These unlicensed traders were an outlaw class of men who, all during the French trading period in America, were a never-ending headache to the authorities. The government felt that trade could be kept more orderly—as well as more profitable for those in charge—if it were confined to the hands of a few big companies who did all their trading at Montreal; but contrary to order after order, these lawless fellows continued to sneak into the wilderness to obtain the furs of the Indians, and the government never succeeded in working out a satisfactory way of dealing with them. If it became severe in its punishments, the wood-rangers would carry their furs to English trading posts, where they might join these rivals of the French—as happened in the case of the first post of the Hudson's Bay Co., in 1670. All efforts to put an end to their practices were in vain, particularly since some of the most prominent French merchants were eager to get their furs; and even the governor, at times, secretly shared in the profits obtained in this way. So to the end of the French regime, the King and his ministers continued to waver in their policy between empty threats of severity and promises of forgiveness.

Michigan's First Prohibition Law

However, these lawless traders were only one of the difficulties of the settlement. Another source of trouble was the ever-present problem of liquor. The missionaries were on the verge of despair because of the suffering, brawling and general disorder caused among the Indians when they drank brandy; and, in desperation, they appealed to the King of France, who ruled that the transportation of liquor to Michilimackinac for unrestricted sale, was to be prohibited. In this way, what is now the Great Lakes region was placed under the ban of its first prohibition law. However, this first liquor law appears to have been no more successful than a similar one which followed it more than two hundred years later. For the Indians promptly began to carry their furs to the English trading posts on Hudson Bay and at Albany, N. Y., where they could get rum as long as their furs held out. The tribesmen liked the taste of French brandy more than that of English rum, but since their chief purpose in drinking liquor was to get drunk, the matter of taste wasn't of much importance to them. Furthermore, rum was cheaper than brandy; making it possible to get as drunk on the price of a mink-skin as they could on a more highly-priced beaver-skin, when they drank brandy.

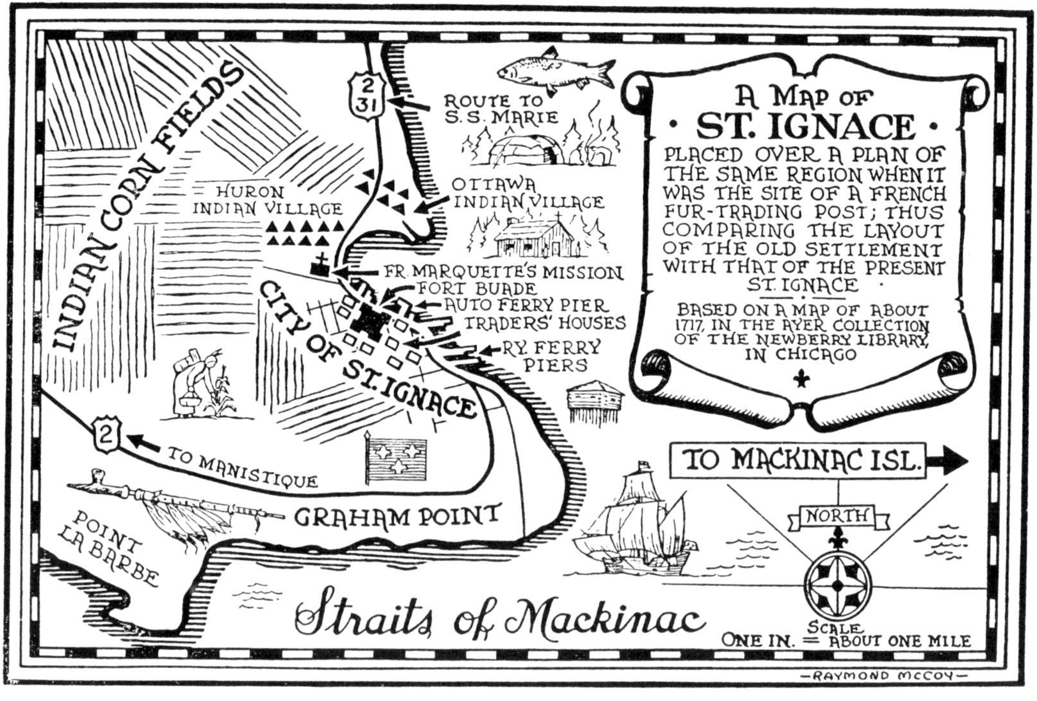
A MAP OF
• ST. IGNACE •
PLACED OVER A PLAN OF THE SAME REGION WHEN IT WAS THE SITE OF A FRENCH FUR-TRADING POST; THUS COMPARING THE LAYOUT OF THE OLD SETTLEMENT WITH THAT OF THE PRESENT ST. IGNACE.
BASED ON A MAP OF ABOUT 1717, IN THE AYER COLLECTION OF THE NEWBERRY LIBRARY, IN CHICAGO
INDIAN CORN FIELDS
HURON INDIAN VILLAGE
2
31
ROUTE TO S.S. MARIE
OTTAWA INDIAN VILLAGE
FR. MARQUETTE'S MISSION
FORT BUADE
AUTO FERRY PIER
TRADERS' HOUSES
RY. FERRY PIERS
CITY OF ST. IGNACE
2
TO MANISTIQUE
GRAHAM POINT
POINT LA BARBE
TO MACKINAC ISL.
NORTH
Straits of Mackinac
SCALE
ONE IN. = ABOUT ONE MILE
—RAYMOND MCCOY—

Cadillac bitterly opposed the brandy ordinance, on the grounds that it caused a loss of trade to the English; and many clashes took place between him and the Jesuits, who advocated the restriction. Reinforcing his position by a health appeal, Cadillac argued, with the air of authority of a radio announcement for patent medicine, that since fish and smoked meat formed the principal food of the inhabitants of Michilimackinac,—a diet which was believed to be unwholesome—"a drink of brandy, after the repast, seems necessary to cook the bilious meats and the crudities which they leave in the stomach. The atmosphere is penetrating and corrosive, and without the brandy they use in the morning, sickness would be much more frequent."

On one occasion during a dispute on the brandy question, Cadillac claims that the Jesuit, Father Carheil, tried to provoke him to an act of violence in order to bring charges against him. The Jesuit rebuked the commandant for his views and policies, to which Cadillac replied that he was only carrying out his orders. The priest rejoined that he ought to obey God and not man, "on which," Cadillac says, "I told him that his talk smelt of sedition a hundred yards off, and begged that he would amend it. He told me that I gave myself airs that did not belong to me, holding his fist before my nose at the same time. I confess I almost forgot that he was a priest, and felt for a moment like knocking his jaw out of joint; but, thank God, I contented myself with taking him by the arm, pushing him out, and ordering him not to come back." Such being the state of affairs between the commandant and the Jesuits, it is not surprising to find Cadillac, on one hand, complaining that he could not get absolution for his sins when he went to confession, and the priests, on the other, denouncing the morals and manners of

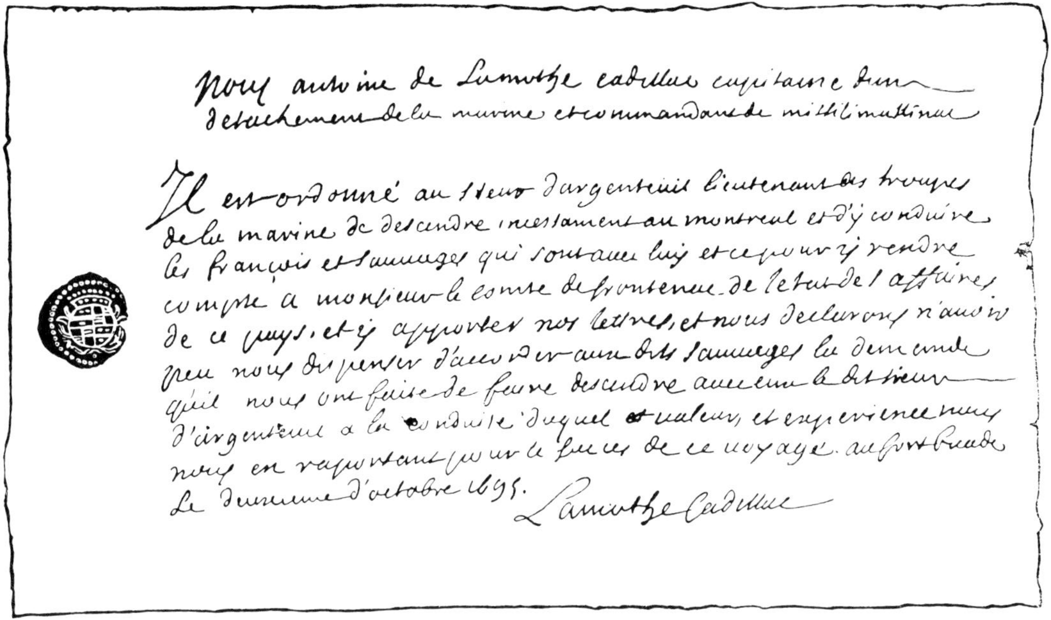

Nous antoine de Lamothe cadillac capitaine dun
detachement dela marine et commandant de michilimakinac

Il est ordonné au sieur dargenteuil lieutenant des troupes
dela marine de descendre incessament au montreal et d'y conduire
les françois et sauvages qui sont avec luy et ce pour y rendre
compte a monsieur le comte de frontenac de letat des affaires
de ce pays, et y apporter nos lettres, et nous declarons n'avoir
peu nous dispenser d'accorder aux dits sauvages la demande
quil nous ont faite de faire descendre avec eux le dit sieur
d'argenteuil a la conduite duquel et valeur, et experience nous
nous en raportant pour le succes de ce voyage. au fort buade
Le deuxieme d'octobre 1695.

Lamothe Cadillac

This is an order issued by Cadillac, in his own handwriting, while he was serving as commandant of the post of Michilimackinac (St. Ignace), in October, 1695. The original manuscript of the above is in the Burton Collection, Detroit.

the settlement in the severest terms.

To the priests themselves, the prohibition on brandy was by no means an unmixed blessing; for in causing the Indians to trade with the English, their converts were thus exposed to the teachings of a rival sect of Christianity, the protestant Church of England. And in those days the teachings of this institution were regarded by Roman Catholics with as much horror as they regard the teachings of Communists today.

Trouble with Iroquois and English

To add to the difficulties within the community, troubles were increasing from without, due in part to the scheming of the Huron Indians of the settlement, who had lost confidence in the French and were dickering with the Iroquois tribes and the English, of New York. The Iroquois were trying to persuade the Indians around the Great Lakes to abandon the French and to do all their trading with them and the English, who gave them a better price for their furs; and Cadillac soon discovered that the tribesmen of St. Ignace were receiving messengers from the Iroquois.

In one instance, seven Iroquois were brought to Michilimackinac in the disguise of prisoners taken by the Hurons; and a Frenchman, suspecting them to be agents of negotiation, stabbed two of the Iroquois as they landed on the beach. The Hurons of the settlement took arms to defend the others, but at length gave one of them, a chief, to the French, who resolved "to make an example of him." They invited the Ottawa Indians to "drink the broth of the Iroquois," who was made fast to a stake, and a Frenchman began to torture him with a red-hot gun barrel. By this means the tribesmen were worked up to the required pitch of ferocity, when they joined in the orgy, which ended by cutting the victim to pieces and eating him. On another occasion, four Iroquois were tortured at St. Ignace at once, and Cadillac wrote: "If any more prisoners are brought to me, I promise you that their fate will be no sweeter."

The French felt that the more the Huron and Ottawa Indians could be persuaded to burn members of the Iroquois tribe, the less danger there would be of a treaty of friendship with the Iroquois, resulting in a loss of the fur trade—the life-blood of Canada. And so determined were the French upon following this policy that on one occasion, a few years previously (in 1690), even the Jesuit missionary of St. Ignace was induced to take a hand in causing the Hurons to "put the Iroquois into the kettle" in order to wreck a treaty that was in prospect. For although the French desired a state of peace between the Iroquois and the Great Lakes tribes, they did not want them to become close friends. A war might interrupt the fur trade, but a state of friendship produced almost the same result by diverting trade to the English and Iroquois. This was a delicate relationship to preserve, and the French were often hard driven for means to continue it.

Conflict Among Authorities

Things generally were in an uproar; because added to the sources of discord and anxiety already mentioned, there was still another problem to cause unrest among the French at Michilimackinac. For over fifty years two conflicting aims divided those who influenced the policies of the French government in Canada. On one side there were the governor and his friends who favored developing the western country by building forts and trading posts along the Great Lakes, and elsewhere in the interior, to advance French interests —and to insure themselves a share in the profits of the fur trade. To give up these posts, they argued, would be the same as handing the country, and the rich fur trade, over to the English. Opposed to this policy were the intendant (an officer who was the King's overseer and a sort of co-governor of Canada), the Jesuits, and the farmers and business men around Quebec and Montreal. These people held that the interior posts should be abandoned and the Indians urged to bring their furs to Montreal for trading, the way they did originally. This should be done, they declared, instead of permitting the young Frenchmen to leave the settlements along the St. Lawrence River—where they were needed on the farms—to go into the Indian country and become ruined by the lawless life of the wilderness and, by their bad example, to wreck the efforts of the missionaries who were trying to Christianize the Indians.

Michilimackinac Abandoned

At length, in 1696, after endless arguing pro and con, the King, influenced by his wife and his Jesuit confessor, and also by the fact that the markets were then flooded with beaver skins, decided in favor of those who urged giving up the trading posts; and he revoked the licenses of all traders, and ordered the soldiers withdrawn from the Great Lakes posts. Any traders caught returning to the interior were warned that they would be condemned to slavery in the galleys. As a result of this decree, Cadillac was recalled as commandant in 1697, and by 1698—except for the Jesuit missionaries, who were permitted to remain in the country—Michilimackinac was abandoned by the French; and the Straits Region was destined to remain without a garrison of soldiers for the next fourteen years. But regardless of what may have been said in defense of this action by the King, affairs around the Great Lakes were such that his order had not been long in effect when wood-rangers, or bootleg traders, were again sneaking into the interior; the French fur trade was being threatened by the English and Iroquois, and the need for withdrawing the King's order—at least in part—soon became evident.

Cadillac Founds City of Detroit

A number of years before, the English and Dutch, from New York, had first begun to make their way up Lake Huron by way of the Detroit River, to take trade away from the French and to talk the local Indians into siding with them and their Iroquois friends against the French. The latter had taken action to stop these activities by having Daniel Greysolon Duluth (a noted French explorer and a former commandant at Michilimackinac, after whom Duluth, Minn., is named), build a fort on the present site of Port Huron (in 1686); but this post was shortly abandoned.

Now, the French hold on the fur trade of the Great Lakes was again being threatened by these rivals, and Cadillac, following his recall from St. Ignace, began to promote a plan to block their further encroachments—and, at the same time, to improve his own worldly affairs. After leaving his rude log settlement in the depths of a savage wilderness at Michilimackinac, he made the long, sailing-ship voyage to France; where, amid the pomp and splendors of the King's palace at Versailles, he applied for and was granted permission to build a fort on the Detroit River, by means of which he hoped to accomplish his purpose. This new post, which was begun in July, 1701, was named Fort Pontchartrain, in honor of the French colonial minister; and it served as the beginning of the modern city of Detroit. Cadillac

Probable appearance of the fort which Cadillac built on the present site of Detroit, in 1701, after his recall as commandant of the post at Michilimackinac (St. Ignace). In 1763, when the fort at Detroit was besieged by Pontiac and his warriors, it was much larger than it is shown here.

resolved to make this place the center of French activities west of Montreal and, by teaching agriculture and the French language to the Indians, and by encouraging them to intermarry with the French inhabitants, he planned to build up the community into a sizeable colony, of which he would be the governor. With this purpose in mind, he enticed the Indians of Michilimackinac to move their homes down to his new settlement on the Detroit River.

Mission of St. Ignace Destroyed

As a result, Michilimackinac soon became almost deserted. In despair at this turn of events, and losing all hope of reforming the lawless wood-rangers who dominated what remained of the settlement, the missionaries burned their house and chapel, in 1705, and journeyed to Quebec. They returned for a few years, but eventually St. Ignace was abandoned entirely as a center of activity of white men. In time, the forest closed in upon the site of the little wilderness community,—the scene of many stirring events—and the location of Father Marquette's grave and mission became unknown to living men.

Finding of Marquette's Probable Grave

More than one hundred and sixty years went by; and then, in May, 1877, Patrick Murray (the father of David Murray), of St. Ignace, was clearing a piece of land to make a garden. The ground was covered by a thick growth of balsam, spruce and pine trees, such as are seen on the hills around St. Ignace today. When the work of clearing had been finished, a flat limestone foundation was exposed to view, measuring thirty-six by forty feet, and of a type such as was commonly used in lining up old log buildings. Within the ground this foundation enclosed, large trees had been stand-

Jacques Marquette

Monument in Marquette Park, St. Ignace, Mich., marking what is quite probably the site of Father Marquette's grave, and the former location of his Indian mission of St. Ignace. In 1877, two hundred years after Marquette was buried beneath the floor of his mission, the remains of a birch-bark coffin and several pieces of human bone were found on this site by Father Edward Jacker and Mr. Patrick Murray, in a grave located within the enclosure of the stone foundation of an old building.

ing, indicating that many years had passed since a building occupied the site. Familiar, as he was, with the history of the region, and with an old French and Indian tradition which related that "a great bishop" was buried at the head of the little bay (East Moran Bay), Mr. Murray consulted Father Edward Jacker, the parish priest of St. Ignace at the time. Father Jacker compared the site with that indicated as the location of the Jesuit mission on La Hontan's map of St. Ignace of 1688, and with the description of Marquette's burial, in the Jesuit Relations reports of 1677. Excavating was begun, and some pieces of birch-bark —apparently the remains of an Indian coffin— along with several fragments of charred bone, were found in a grave located within the space enclosed by the foundation. The fragments of bone were identified by Dr. Pommier, a physician and surgeon of Cheboygan, as "undoubtedly human, and bearing the marks of fire." It was accordingly concluded, from this evidence, that Father Marquette's grave had been found; and that the excavated pieces of bone and birch-bark represented all that remained of the renowned missionary-explorer, and the birch-bark coffin in which his bones had been buried almost exactly two hundred years before. At the time of their discovery, a part of the excavated fragments of bone were sent to the Jesuits of Marquette University, Milwaukee, Wis.; while the rest were returned to the grave in which they were found. This is marked today by a monument (erected in 1882), in Marquette Park, only a few yards off the main highway running through St. Ignace.

Fort Erected on Mackinaw City Site

About fourteen years after the founding of Detroit, due to the appeals of the missionaries, and to the natural advantages of the place as a station

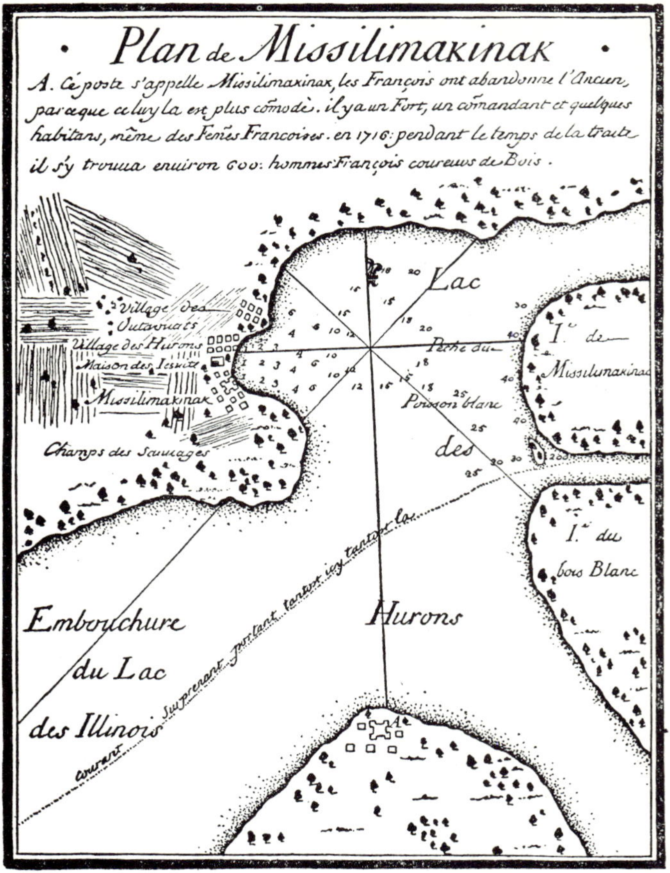

This is an old French map of the Straits of Mackinac region, which is believed to have been made sometime about 1717. The explanatory lines above (which are only a part of the lengthy legend on the original map), are in French, and a translation reads: "This post is called Missilimakinak, the French have abandoned the old fort [*at St. Ignace*] *because this one* [*that is, the one at Mackinaw City, marked "A"*] *is more convenient. There is a fort, a commandant, a few settlers, and even some French women. In 1716, during trading time, there were gathered at the fort about 600 French wood-rangers." The original map is in the Edward E. Ayer Collection, of the Newberry Library, Chicago.*

for trade, the French reopened the trading post on the Straits of Mackinac. However, instead of continuing it at St. Ignace, they began an entirely new settlement on the south side of the Straits because they found this location to be "plus comode," or more convenient. This new post—the second in the Straits Region—was erected on the site of the present Michilimackinac State Tourist Park—a spot sometimes called Old Mackinaw, and known to the Indians as *Pequotenong*, or headland,—in the present Mackinaw City. It was begun at a time when trade was to be interrupted, off and on, for about twenty years, by a series of wars between the French and the Fox Indians of Wisconsin; and later, by the goings and comings of Indian war parties during the French and Indian War, between France and England. During this latter war, large bands of Indians gave up their hunting of fur-bearing animals for the fur trade, to assemble at Michilimackinac and be led by Charles de Langlade, a native half-breed, to the place of battle, where they took part in the defeat of General Braddock; the siege and subsequent massacre of Fort William Henry; an engagement with the rangers of Major Robert Rogers, in which Rogers was wounded; and in the decisive battle on the Plains of Abraham, at Quebec.

However, in spite of the interruptions in trade caused by these wars, Michilimackinac again became a busy center of the French fur trade—a serious rival of Detroit; and it continued as such until the close of the French and Indian War, in 1760. At that time, the French and English—who had been at war almost continuously, both in America and in Europe, about one thing or another, for over fifty years—finally settled their rival claims to the soil and fur trade of North America, when the defeated French were forced to surrender Michilimackinac, as well as most of their other possessions in America, to the English.

(In its larger aspects, the outcome of this long struggle, between France and England, has had a profound effect on the language, religion, government and business conditions of the people now living in the United States and Canada. It decided that the majority of these people were to be English-speaking Protestants, living under a representative government with liberal opportunities for individual enterprise; rather than French-speaking Roman Catholics, whose traditions of government were those of an absolute monarchy with strict government control of all activities. Hence, in settling the fate of the greater part of a continent, this is one of the most important struggles recorded in history.)

Scene of Indian Massacre

The English had scarcely occupied their recently-won posts when the native Indian inhabitants, dissatisfied with their new rulers, arose in rebellion, incited by Chief Pontiac, in the spring of 1763. During this uprising the Indians captured eight of the thirteen forts they attacked, Detroit being the only post west of Niagara which did not fall. *And it is the part of this Indian outbreak that took place at this second settlement of Fort Michilimackinac (Mackinaw City), which serves as the subject of the narrative related in the following chapter—the massacre of the English of Fort Michilimackinac.*

Major Robert Rogers at Michilimackinac

After the Indian massacre, peaceful relations were restored between the English and the Indians, in the autumn of 1764, upon the arrival of Captain William Howard and a detachment of troops. Captain Howard remained as commandant for about two years, and he was succeeded by the famous colonial ranger, Major Robert Rogers,—the hero of Kenneth Roberts' novel "Northwest Passage"—who had distinguished himself during the fighting in the French and Indian War, and in the struggle around Detroit in the Chief Pontiac War. Rogers, accompanied by his wife, reached Fort Michilimackinac in August, 1766, and he at once embarked upon a policy which was to get him into serious trouble.

Search for Northwest Passage

However, while Rogers' period of service at Fort Michilimackinac is marked chiefly by the difficulties he had with his superiors, the phase of his activities at Michilimackinac that is perhaps better known is his attempt to find the semi-fabulous Northwest Passage, a cross-country waterway to the Pacific Ocean, which had been eagerly sought after for many years as an aid to commerce between Europe and Asia. In the fall of 1766, an expedition with this end in view set out from Fort Michilimackinac. It was commanded by one of Rogers' old comrades in the rangers, Captain James Tute, who was designated as "Commanding a party for the Discovery of the North West Passage from the Atlantick into the Passifick Ocean, if any such Passage there be, or for the discovery of the River Ourigan that falls into the Pacifick Ocean about the Latitude Fifty."

The undertaking proved a failure; the members of the expedition proceeding only as far as Grand Portage, on the northwestern shore of Lake Superior (near the present site of Fort William, Ontario), from where the party returned to Michilimackinac because of the shortage of food—"no Provision nor goods to get any with." However, a

Major Robert Rogers, the famous colonial ranger, and the hero of Kenneth Roberts' novel "Northwest Passage," who served as commandant of Fort Michilimackinac (Mackinaw City) in 1766-67. This drawing is from a portrait of Rogers published in London in 1776. The signature is from one of his letters in the W. L. Clements Library, Ann Arbor.

book written by the map-maker of the enterprise, Captain Jonathan Carver, concerning his travels, was so successful that it aroused European interest in America more than any book had been able to do up to that time. (The coast-to-coast airlines, railroads, and highways which traverse North America today represent the present-day outgrowth of this long quest for a route from the Atlantic to the Pacific.)

Rogers' Indian Conference

When Rogers came to Fort Michilimackinac, he had orders from General Gage and Sir William Johnson,—the latter being head of the department of Indian affairs—to confine trade to the fort area in order that the cheating of the Indians, and the debauching of them with rum, might be prevented. But Rogers felt—and with good reason—that if the traders were not allowed to go into the Indian hunting-grounds, the amount of trade would be greatly reduced, since many of the western tribesmen would not make the long trip to Michilimackinac, but would do their trading with the French, who were still in the Mississippi country.

Aware of the far-off position of Fort Michilimackinac from headquarters, Rogers knew that he could not be closely watched; so he decided to run the post according to his own ideas. In this he was encouraged by the traders, who stood to profit by such a policy. Contrary to orders to economize, he spent large sums of money for Indian presents to win the friendship of the tribesmen. And to prevent the outbreak of a threatening war between the Ojibwa and Sioux tribes,—which would have disrupted trade—Rogers held a great peace conference at Fort Michilimackinac, in the spring of 1767. This conference was attended by one of the largest gatherings of Indians ever held on the North American continent. The woods for a considerable distance around the fort was crowded with Indian lodges; and before the meeting broke up, Rogers devoted a whole day to giving out presents to the Indians—blankets, knives, guns, hatchets, powder, lead, tobacco, ornaments, etc.—which he obtained from the traders on credit. The Indians were pleased, but Rogers was paving the way for trouble for himself.

Rogers in Trouble

Towards the close of June (1767), while this great conference was in full swing, a commissary of Indian affairs, sent out by Sir William Johnson, arrived at Michilimackinac to watch what was going on. This commissary was Lieutenant Benjamin Roberts, a retired army officer—and one of Johnson's favorites—who held a grudge against Rogers because of a quarrel which took place between the two men at the Indian peace conference held at Oswego, N. Y., the previous year. Roberts' instructions were to watch expenses and to enforce trading regulations, the latter including some restrictions on the sale of rum. Efforts were constantly being made to smuggle rum out of the fort because it was a highly profitable item of trade,—particularly so when diluted with water—and in his efforts to uphold these regulations, Roberts frequently came into conflict with Rogers. The already hostile feeling which existed between the two men was made worse when Rogers grew worried and moody because his superiors refused to pay the bills he had contracted. And it was rumored about the community that unless he was used better, and approval was given to his proposed plan to set up a separate government at Michilimackinac,—headed by himself—Rogers intended to desert the post the following spring, and after robbing the neighboring forts, to go and join the French on the Mississippi.

Matters came to a head in the middle of August 1767, when Roberts was awakened in the middle of the night by the noise of some traders smuggling rum out of the fort for Rogers, who had decided to do some trading on his own account in order to pay his bills. The following morning, Roberts obtained a detail of men to go out and bring back the rum, which had been hidden among the bushes on the northern shore of the Straits, on Point St. Ignace. When the kegs of rum—forty-one in number—were returned, a heated dispute arose outside the water gate of the fort, as to what was to be done with them. Roberts wanted the kegs put in the common rum store, while Rogers ordered them placed in the King's Storehouse, and if left unclaimed, to be given to the troops "at times when it's necessary to repair the fort, or when they do other service extraordinary which they have no pay for." During the quarrel, Roberts challenged Rogers to a fight outside the fort area; adding to his challenge, an accusation—based on information given to him by Rogers' secretary, Potter,—that Rogers was a traitor and guilty of high treason. He made this charge before the amazed inhabitants who had been attracted by the disorders. The quarrel ended with Rogers ordering Roberts taken to his house and locked up. Trouble broke out again between the two men, in September, and this time Roberts was put in irons and sent to Montreal for trial.

Meanwhile, Gage and Johnson had become aware of the goings-on at Michilimackinac and had decided to remove Rogers for his extravagance; but upon hearing of the charges of treason, they ordered Lieutenant Spiesmacher, the officer second in command, to put Rogers under arrest "For High Treason, or being a Traitor to his King & Country, &c." As may be imagined, these happenings caused great excitement among the small

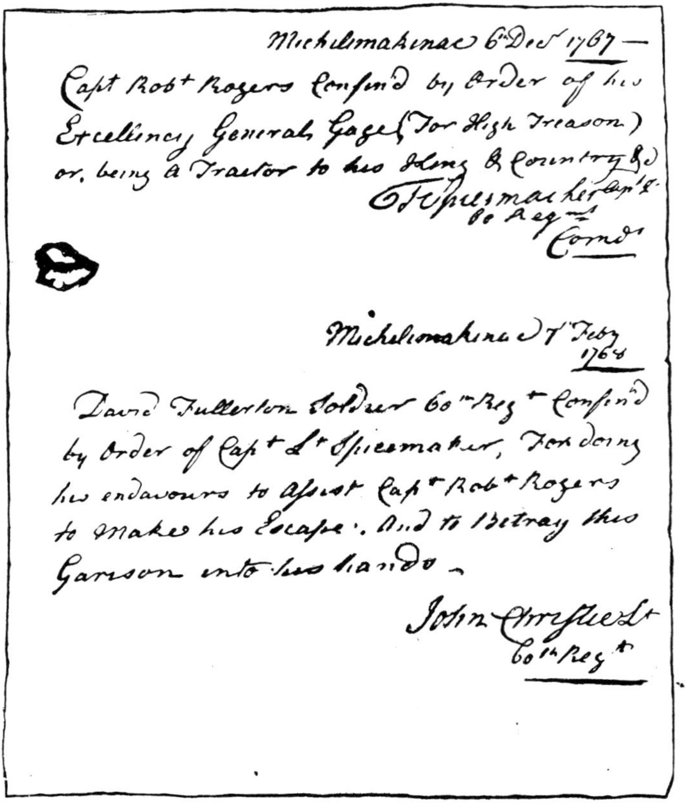

Michilimakinac 6th Decr 1767 —

Capt Robt Rogers Confin'd by Order of his Excellency General Gage (For High Treason) or, being a Traitor to his King & Country &c

G. T. Spiesmacher Capt Lt
60 Regt
Comdt

Michilimakinac 7 Feby 1768

David Fullerton Soldier 60th Regt Confin'd by Order of Capt Lt Spiesmaker, For doing his endavours to Assist Capt Robt Rogers to Make his Escape. And to Betray this Garison into his hands —

John Christie Lt
60th Regt

This is the report sent to General Thomas Gage, chief of the British forces in America, 1763-75, concerning the arrest of the famous colonial ranger, Robert Rogers, while he was serving as commandant of Fort Michilimackinac, in 1767. The report was sent to Gage by Captain-Lieutenant Spiesmacher, the officer second in command at Michilimackinac; and it tells of the arrest also of Rogers' orderly, David Fullerton, who was accused of trying to help Rogers to escape. The original document is in the Gage papers at the W. L. Clements Library.

group of inhabitants at Michilimackinac. The Indians, in particular, were much puzzled and very angry about this treatment of the commandant, and several parties of them came to see Rogers during his imprisonment. Throughout the winter of 1767-68, Rogers was confined and closely guarded; and during this time he wrote to General Gage asking for a speedy trial as "confinement is detrimental to the health of a person of a robust constitution like mine, being always used to marching and a lively exercise."

During this time also, it is alleged that Rogers —aided by his orderly, David Fullerton— tried to obtain assistance to escape from Fort Michilimackinac and to make his way to the French, in Illinois. But the plot was exposed, and in the spring of 1768 he was taken from Fort Michilimackinac to Detroit, in irons. In this ignominious manner departed from the Straits Region Major Robert Rogers, the famous French and Indian War ranger, who less than two years before had come with such great plans for finding the Northwest Passage. "I was thrown," he afterwards testified, "into the hold of the vessel, upon the ballast of stores, still in irons; and in this manner transported the whole distance. When they were taken off the weight of the irons was so considerable, and they were fastened so tightly, that my legs were bent. From the pain I suffered, together with the cold, the bone of my right leg was split and the marrow forced its way out through the skin."

From Detroit Rogers was conveyed to Montreal and tried on a charge of mutiny. However, the evidence against him was but little; and what there was was soon discredited because of the lack of supporting testimony. It is said that the traders, to whom Rogers was indebted, were

Major (later Colonel) Arent Schuyler De Peyster, who, as British commandant of Fort Michilimackinac (1774-79) when the American Revolution broke out, was kept busy in preserving the loyalty of the Indians, and in organizing war parties to march against the Colonists. In 1779 Major De Peyster became lieutenant-governor at Detroit, where he remained in command until 1784. This drawing is based on an oil painting; the autograph is from the Clements Library.

unwilling to testify against him, feeling that they stood a better chance to get their money if he were freed. The case collapsed completely; and in the spring of 1770, Rogers sailed for England, where he spent some time in a debtors' prison. After his release, according to his own story, he passed to the Barbary States, and fought two battles for the Dey of Algiers. During the American Revolution he fought for a brief time on the side of the British, later returning to England, where the remainder of his life was spent.

American Revolution at Mackinac

In 1775, when the American Revolution broke out, Fort Michilimackinac was commanded by Major Arent Schuyler DePeyster, of New York. And although Michilimackinac was far from the actual scene of battle, Major DePeyster was kept busy in preserving the loyalty of the Indians and in gathering war parties to be sent eastward to join General Burgoyne, and other British officers, who were fighting the American colonists. However, in 1779 the war was brought nearer home when the American, Colonel George Rogers Clark, invaded what is now Indiana; captured Fort Sackville, at Vincennes, and threatened to take the forts at Detroit and Michilimackinac. DePeyster then became anxious about the security of his own post, and he wrote to his superior: "The whole country is in the greatest confusion, being at a loss to know which route the rebels will take next." He realized that if Detroit were captured his fort of "rickety pickets," as he called it, would face a "dismal prospect"; however, he set to work strengthening his defenses to prepare for a possible attack by the Americans. Some of the buildings within the fort were torn down and the timber used to reinforce the pickets of the stockade; a

Colonel George Rogers Clark, the American officer, whose invasion of Illinois and Indiana, during the American Revolution, caused the British to move the fort and trading post on the Straits of Mackinac from the southern mainland to Mackinac Island; thus starting a white settlement on the Island. Clark's victories also had much to do with causing the Great Lakes Region to become a part of the United States instead of remaining as a British possession. This drawing is from an oil painting, and the autograph is from the Historical Society of Wisconsin.

platform was also erected to permit the defenders to fire from "a good height through loop holes," while the soldiers' quarters were surrounded with pickets to guard against a possible surprise attack by the Indians trading within the fort.

A few yards southwest of the fort there was a cluster of hills of drift sand, the remains of which are to be seen today behind the row of summer cottages. These were dangerous as possible places of concealment for an attacking party, so the commandant detailed his men to remove them. Only twelve shovels were on hand in the fort, and for a time the best shoveling efforts of the soldiers were offset by wind storms from off Lake Michigan, which would sweep in and build up the hills as fast as they could be reduced. However, through persistent labor, the hills were, at length, partly cut down and the threat from this quarter somewhat removed.

The Fort at Mackinac Island

But still greater precautions were to be taken to save Michilimackinac for the British. In October, 1779, Captain Patrick Sinclair arrived as the new lieutenant governor and superintendent, in response to DePeyster's persistent requests to be relieved from a post he apparently did not like. Sinclair had been assigned to Michilimackinac four years before (in April, 1775), while in England; but as the result of being taken into custody by the Americans upon his arrival in New York, and being forced to return to England, and then to make his way back to America, it took him four and one-half years to reach his post. At Michilimackinac, Sinclair at once became impressed with the superior defensive advantages of Mackinac Island, and he began to arrange for the removal of the fort to this site. However, while doing so, he continued to strengthen the fort on the mainland to

Captain Patrick Sinclair, lieutenant governor ***and super-intendent*** *of Michilimackinac* (1779-82), ***who was the last*** *commandant of the fort on the mainland (Mackinaw City), and the builder of the fort on Mackinac Island. The above was drawn from a silhouette made of Sinclair* ***after he had*** *retired to his home in Scotland. The autograph* ***is from the*** *W. L. Clements* ***Library.***

prepare for a possible attack before the shift to the Island could be made. Among these preparations was the erection of a block house, sixteen feet square, to the south of the fort, "to command the hollow ground behind the sand hills which the troops could not reduce." At length, permission was obtained from the Indians to occupy the Island by paying them five thousand pounds in New York currency (about $12,500) for it; and in 1780-81 the log church and other buildings of the settlement were moved across the Straits to the Island where a new fort and settlement—the third in the Straits Region—were begun. This move was the beginning of a white settlement on Mackinac Island. Without it the Island might not be as well known as it is today.

In making the transfer, care was necessary to conceal from the Indians the real motive for the change; since there was danger that they might regard the action as an indication of fear and timidity; and nobody with these qualities could long hold their respect or influence their behavior. Sinclair therefore explained to the tribesmen that he personally disliked the site on the mainland, a dislike which, he says, "I often express to them."

In describing the site on the Island which he had selected for the new fort, Sinclair asked Captain Brehm, his superior at Detroit, for an engineer to build the stronghold; adding the warning, "But for God's sake be careful in the choice of an engineer and don't send up one of your paper engineers, found of fine regular Polygons." However, as events worked out, there was no need for Sinclair to concern himself about this feature, since it appears that no military engineer was available—"paper engineer," or otherwise—and he found it necessary to lock after all the construction work himself.

Old Fort Mackinac, on Mackinac Island, erected by the British in 1780-83; ***surrendered to Americans,*** 1796; ***retaken by British,*** 1812; ***returned to Americans,*** 1815; ***abandoned by Americans.*** 1895.

To add to the cares and expenses of building a new fort on the Island, and the worry concerning a possible attack by the Americans before the work had been completed, the restless local tribesmen gave the British something more to feel anxious about. With their natural love of plunder and glory, it was contrary to Indian nature to stand idle while there was a war going on around them. And to induce them to side with the British, and take part in raids against the Americans in the Ohio valley, and against the Spaniards along the Mississippi River, Sinclair had to spend so much money for presents that he was finally recalled from the post for his extravagance. The bills he thus incurred continued to plague him for some time after he left Mackinac—even to the extent of landing him in a London debtors' prison for a while.

Old Stockade Reconstructed

After the removal of the fort to the Island, the location on the southern mainland again became a deserted wilderness. And when Mackinaw City was settled, about the middle of the last century, the old fort site became a rendezvous for relic hunters who churned the neighboring soil into a mass of hills and hollows in quest of uniform buttons, knives, beads, musket and cannon balls, forks, spoons, human skeletons, and other objects which had become buried in the ground during the period of about sixty-seven years that the place was occupied by a fort and fur-trading post. Then in 1932, the custodian of the Michilimackinac State Tourist Park was leveling the site for use as a part of the tent and trailer camping-grounds. As his plow turned up the soil, he came upon the rotted and crumbled post ends of the walls of the old fort. And as an outgrowth of the discovery, a sum of money was appropriated by the State of Michigan, and the stockade was reconstructed along the lines of the excavated walls of the ancient stronghold. Because of the lack of funds, it was not possible to rebuild the church and houses which stood inside the original enclosure; however, it is hoped that someday it will be possible to erect a complete replica of old Fort Michilimackinac, somewhat as it is pictured in the center-piece drawing of this book. Such a replica would serve as an historical exhibit which would aid American tourists in gaining a better understanding of the early beginnings of their Nation.

Mackinac Delivered to Americans

Two years after the British took up their position on the Island—in 1783—and before the expected attack had been made, the war with the Colonists ended. And, as a result of the terms of peace, Mackinac became a possession of the United States. However, due to the strong desire of the British to retain the fur trade for themselves, and to the failure of the Americans to carry out the terms of the treaty in regard to the Loyalists (the American colonists opposing the war for independence, who were treated like strike-breakers by those favoring it), the British kept American troops from occupying Mackinac until the late summer of 1796. At this time the British surrendered Fort Mackinac to Major Henry Burbeck and his force of United States regulars, and then took up a position on St. Joseph Island (in the St. Mary's River, half way to Sault Ste. Marie), where they built a new fort (Fort St. Joseph), and awaited their chance to regain Mackinac. As events worked out, the opportunity to do this was not long in coming.

Americans Occupy Mackinac

After the United States gained actual possession of Mackinac and the other posts on the Great Lakes, American fur traders began rushing into the country to share in the profits of trade. However, they soon learned that while a final peace had been arranged, affairs between England and America were still far from settled. For the United States held the military posts, but, by the terms of peace, British traders,—particularly those of the powerful North West and Mackinaw companies—were still allowed to trade in American territory; to mix freely with the Indians of the United States, and by this means to retain virtual control of the tribesmen. This condition led to an intense rivalry between the British and the American traders for the furs of the Indians, and contributed largely to the outbreak of a second war with England in 1812. In that year, the enemies of the fur-bearing animals stopped killing them for a time while they turned to the business of killing one another.

War of 1812 at Mackinac

Because of the importance of its position, Mackinac became involved in the fighting which ensued, serving as the scene of two encounters between the British and the Americans during the war. The first of these encounters took place on July 17, 1812, when the British, from Fort St. Joseph, and about six hundred of their Indian allies, surprised the feeble American garrison — who had not been notified that war had begun—by landing on the Island, in the middle of the night, at the point known since as British Landing. Commanded by Captain Charles Roberts, a veteran who had seen service in Europe and Asia,—a relative of Lord Roberts of World War I fame—they hauled a gun up to the heights

A Map of
MACKINAC
ISLAND
MICHIGAN
In the Straits of
Mackinac Region
Point Aux Pins
British Landing
Scott's Cave Road
Tranquil Bluff View Trail
Swamp Trail
Site of Old Early Farm
State Road
Partridge Trail
Battlefield of Aug. 4, 1814
Eagle Point Cave
British Landing Road
Lake Shore Road
Wawashkamo Golf Course
Crack In Island
Cave of the Woods
Early Trail
Leslie Ave.
Short Cut Trail
Annex Road
Tranquil Lane
Reese Road
Indian Road
Garrison Road
Tranquil Trail
Old Fort Garden
Leslie Ave.
Crooked Tree Drive
Sugar Loaf Road
Lime Trail
Ft. Holmes Rd
Cupid's Pathway
Cemeteries Road
Huron Road
Custer Road
Grand Golf Course
Old Rifle Range
Deer Park
Old Lime Kiln
Sugar Loaf Rock
Arch Rock Trail
Arch Rock Rd.
Lake Shore Road
Cadotte Ave.
Wisnebago Trail
Huron Road
Manito Trail
Boat Piers
LAKE HURON
LAKE HURON
Arch Rock Natural Bridge
Robinson's Folly Cliff
Fort Mackinac, 1781 - 1895
Old Mission Church, Built 1830.
NORTH
SOUTH
EAST
WEST
① Old Fort Mackinac
② Marquette Park
③ Old Astor Fur House
④ Grand Hotel
⑤ Old Mission Church
⑥ Robinson's Folly Cliff
⑦ Arch Rock
⑧ Skull Cave
⑨ Point Lookout
⑩ Fort Holmes
⑪ Sugar Loaf Rock
⑫ Scott's Cave
¼ Mile
½ Mile
One Mile
Distance Scale
Raymond McCoy

(now Fort Holmes), commanding the rear of Fort Mackinac. And the next morning they forced the helpless American commandant.—Lieutenant Porter Hanks, whose "fifty-seven effective men" were greatly outnumbered—to surrender without the firing of a shot. This was the opening blow of the War of 1812. It caused the Indians—who always preferred a winner—to flock to the side of the British, and in this way, had a direct effect on the subsequent surrender of Detroit by General Hull "to save the women and children from the scalping knives of the Indians." The loss of Mackinac also had a direct bearing on the massacre of the American garrison at Fort Dearborn, now Chicago.

British Build Fort George, now Fort Holmes

Once more in possession of Mackinac, the British, with the aid of forced labor from the inhabitants, built a new fort on the high land to the rear of Fort Mackinac, in order to protect themselves against a maneuver such as they had just executed against the Americans. They called this stronghold Fort George, in honor of King George, the Third, the reigning monarch of England.

The second military engagement of the war was on August 4, 1814,—a battle fought in the clearing of the old Early Farm, in the northern part of the Island and known as the Battle of Mackinac Island. In this encounter, the Americans—suffering fifteen killed and fifty-two wounded, including the loss of a valuable officer, Major Andrew Hunter Holmes,—tried unsuccessfully to dislodge the British and Indians from the Island.

Failing to take the Island by assault, the Americans decided to try to starve the British garrison into surrender. Two of the five ships in the attack ing party, the "Scorpion" and "Tigress,"—ships which had taken part in Perry's victory of the Battle of Lake Erie, the previous year—were detailed to blockade Mackinac. And, as time went on, the blockade became so effective that the price of bread on Mackinac Island is reported to have risen to one dollar a loaf; while the garrison was placed on a diet consisting mainly of salted horse meat and fish. At length, when reduced to the point of starvation, the British resolved to make an attempt to capture the blockading vessels. A party set out from the Island, consisting of about one hundred men in five open boats and canoes, carrying two small cannon. On the dark and cloudy night of September 3, 1814, they swept down on the "Tigress," then somewhere near Detour, about thirty-five miles northeast of Mackinac Island. They managed to come within fifty yards of her before they were sighted and fired upon by the ship's crew; and before the vessel's guns could be reloaded, the British clambered over her sides. A brief, sharp, hand-to-hand struggle followed, during which the crew of thirty Americans was subdued and made prisoners.

Two days later, the "Scorpion"—which had been separated from the "Tigress" for several days—was seen working up to join her companion ship, her American crew entirely unaware of what had happened. When night fell, she anchored a short distance away; and early the next morning the "Tigress" with her British captors still flying the American flag, bore down on the "Scorpion." When within ten yards of her the British leaped out of hiding—fired a volley of musketry at her surprised crew—quickly drew along side, and in a few minutes were in possession of the ship and her men.

Mackinac Returned to Americans

The capture of the blockading vessels marked the failure of the Americans in their attempt to re-take the Island with their armed forces. However, at the close of the war, in 1815, Mackinac was returned to the United States by the treaty of peace; so what the Americans could not accomplish with their army and navy, their diplomats gained by negotiation.

After the Americans regained possession of the Island, the name of the fort which the British had erected on the heights above Fort Mackinac, was changed from Fort George to Fort Holmes, in honor of Major Andrew Hunter Holmes, who was killed in the battle on the Island in August, 1814. Later, Fort Holmes was demolished; and in 1936 a replica of it was erected on the same site, based on plans obtained from Washington.

John Jacob Astor's Fur Company

When peace was restored, John Jacob Astor—who had organized his American Fur Co. in 1808 to compete with the large British North West and Mackinaw companies—induced the United States Congress to restrict all trade within the borders of the United States to American citizens. And during the American trading period which followed, the commerce in furs continued to increase in volume until it reached the highest point of its development. With the western headquarters of Astor's giant Fur Company located on the Island, Mackinac became the center of one of the most powerful trading firms in the country. Its numerous district trading posts and employees were to be found on the smallest waterways of the Great Lakes, the Mississippi and the Missouri Rivers, and as far west as the Yellowstone River in Montana and Wyoming.

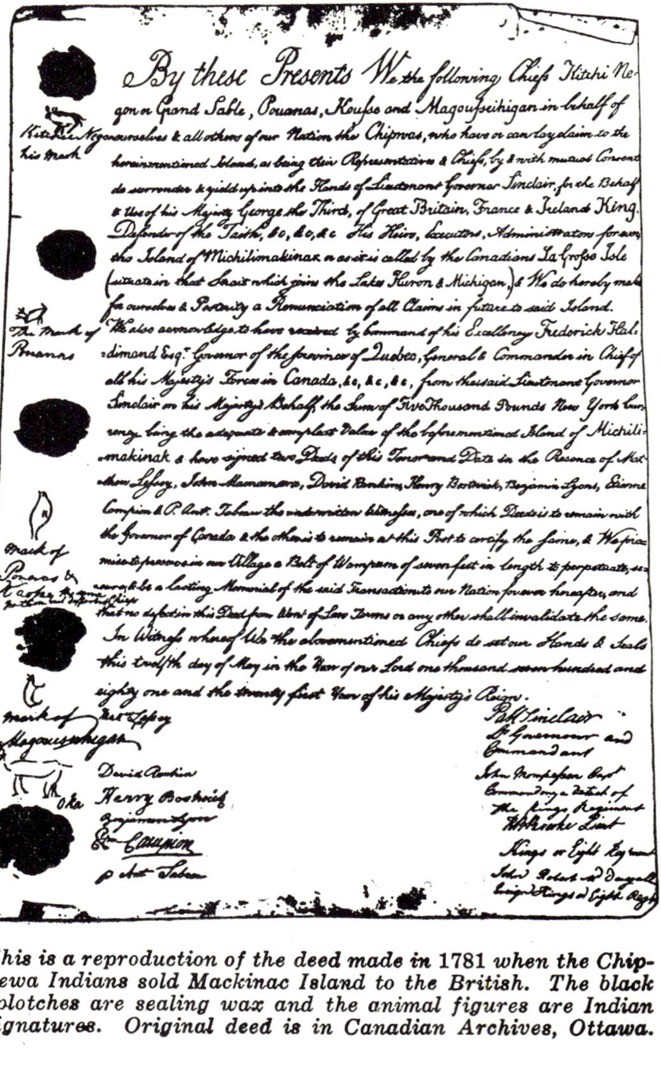

By these Presents We the following Chiefs Kitchi Negon or Grand Sable, Pouanas, Koufse and Magoufseihigan in behalf of ourselves & all others of our Nation the Chipwas, who have or can lay claim to the hereinmentioned Island, as being their Representatives & Chiefs, by & with mutual Consent do surrender & yield up into the Hands of Lieutenant Governor Sinclair, for the Behalf & Use of his Majesty George the Third, of Great Britain, France & Ireland King, Defender of the Faith, &c, &c, &c His Heirs, Executors, Administrators for ever, the Island of Michilimakinak or as it is called by the Canadians La Grosse Isle (situate in that Strait which joins the Lakes Huron & Michigan,) & We do hereby make for ourselves & Posterity a Renunciation of all Claims in future to said Island. We also acknowledge to have received by Command of his Excellency Frederick Haldimand Esqr. Governor of the Province of Quebec, General & Commander in Chief of all his Majesty's Forces in Canada, &c, &c, &c, from the said Lieutenant Governor Sinclair on his Majesty's Behalf the Sum of Five Thousand Pounds New York Currency being the adequate & compleat Value of the beforementioned Island of Michilimakinak & have signed two Deeds of this Tenor and Date in the Presence of Matthew Lessey, John Macnamara, David Rankin, Henry Bostwick, Benjamin Lyons, Etienne Campion & P. Ant. Tabeau the underwritten Witnesses, one of which Deeds is to remain with the Governor of Canada & the other is to remain at this Post to certify the same, & We promise to preserve in our Village a Belt of Wampum of seven feet in length to perpetuate, secure & be a lasting Memorial of the said Transaction to our Nation for ever hereafter, and that no defect in this Deed from Want of Law Terms or any other shall invalidate the same. In Witness whereof We the abovementioned Chiefs do set our Hands & Seals this twelfth day of May in the Year of our Lord one thousand seven hundred and eighty one and the twenty first Year of his Majesty's Reign.

Kitchie Negon his Mark

The Mark of Pouanas

Mark of Ponaas & Kaofse

mark of Magousseihigan

Oka

Matt Lessey

David Rankin

Henry Bostwick

Benjamin Lyon

Etn Campion

P Ant Tabeau

Patt Sinclair Lt Governour and Commandant

John Mompesson Capt Commanding a Detach of the Kings Regiment

Wm Brooke Lieut Kings or Eight Regiment

John Robert McDougall Ensign Kings or Eight Regt

This is a reproduction of the deed made in 1781 when the Chippewa Indians sold Mackinac Island to the British. The black splotches are sealing wax and the animal figures are Indian signatures. Original deed is in Canadian Archives, Ottawa.

Although Astor himself never set foot on Mackinac Island, he managed through Ramsey Crooks and Robert Stuart, his agents in the Great Lakes region, to introduce new and improved methods of trade, and to organize his company along the greedy and ruthless lines which were common among business men in those days. The Indians were made drunk so that their hard-earned winter's catch of furs might be obtained for almost nothing; employees were engaged for such small pay that they were always in debt to the Fur Company's store, and thus were made virtual slaves of the firm; and every other known device was used to increase the Company's profits. In the wild country where the United States had but few soldiers, the Fur Company's agents went heavily armed; government representatives were defied; and rival traders were browbeaten and eliminated from competition by whatever means were deemed necessary, even by outright murder.

Astor America's Richest Man

In this way the American Fur Company gained a virtual monopoly of the rich trade in furs. And when he died, in 1848, at the age of eighty-four, John Jacob Astor—who had come to America as John Jakob Ashdour, a poor immigrant boy from Germany,—was, by far, the richest man in America. His fortune—increased considerably by investments in New York real estate—was estimated at twenty millions of dollars. His sordid business methods—which were not far different from those of other business men of his time—appear to have had the hearty approval of the respectable people of those days; for most of the newspaper accounts of his death were filled with praise of him and his deeds. And we are told by Washington Irving, in his essay "Astoria," that Astor was "a man whose name and character are worthy of being

John Jacob Astor, founder of the great Astor fortune, who acquired most of his early wealth in the buying and selling of furs. The greater part of these furs were handled through the western headquarters of Astor's American Fur Co., on Mackinac Island. This drawing is from a painting; the signature is from the Yale University Library.

enrolled in the history of commerce as illustrating its noblest aims and soundest maxims." Apparently the only dissenting voice was that of the famous newspaperman, James Gordon Bennett,—the promoter of Stanley's search for Livingstone—who wrote in his New York *Herald:* "He [Astor] has exhibited, at best, but the ingenious powers of a self-invented money-making machine . . . without turning it to any permanent benefit to that community [New York City] from whose industry he obtained half the amount of his fortune."

Doctor Beaumont and Alexis St. Martin

In June, 1822, during the bustle and money-making of the American fur-trading days, a young canoeman of the American Fur Company was wounded on the Island by the accidental discharge of a shot gun. And as an outgrowth of the mishap, Mackinac Island became linked with the first important American contribution to the science of medicine. The wounded man, Alexis St. Martin, was in the stone basement of the Fur Company's retail store (now the Early Cottage, at the base of the fort hill) when the gun went off, only about three feet from his body. A large hole was torn in his side; but to the amazement of Dr. William Beaumont, the surgeon from Fort Mackinac, who attended him, St. Martin recovered. However, the hole in his stomach stubbornly resisted all efforts to make it close. The injured man had to wear a bandage over this opening to retain his food; and in time, this bandage was replaced by a natural growth of stomach tissue which formed to cover the opening. However, this growth was fastened only along the upper edge of the hole, and in such a way that it could be pushed back with the finger, like a trap door or lid. For this

Dr. William Beaumont, Surgeon of Fort Mackinac, in 1822, whose experiments on Alexis St. Martin, a wounded Mackinac fur trader, resulted in the world's first scientific ***description of the processes of digestion. This drawing is based on*** *a portrait provided by the American Medical Association;* ***the autograph is from the Clements Library.***

reason the bantering villagers and fur-traders called St. Martin "the man with a lid on his stomach."

When this "lid", or growth of stomach tissue, was pushed back, Dr. Beaumont could peer inside and see the living stomach while it was digesting food. Although punctures of the stomach had been observed before, much guess-work went on as to what takes place inside the organ during the processes of digestion. Aware of the value of his opportunity, Dr. Beaumont began a series of experiments which he continued for several years—interrupted at various times when St. Martin became homesick and ran off on him. During these years of experimenting he was transferred from post to post, the last being Fort Crawford, at the present site of Prairie du Chien, Wis. He inserted various kinds of food, tied to silk threads, into the stomach, and by pulling them out at intervals, he was able to learn how long it takes to digest each kind. He put a rubber tube into the stomach and siphoned off a small glassful of pure gastric juice, a fluid secreted by the stomach; and he found that food placed in this glass was "digested," or dissolved, almost the same as when it was placed in the stomach. He also observed other facts about the stomach and digestion—including the fact that St. Martin's digestion was not so good after he had been on a spree, or when he was angered by the villagers and fur-traders, who made fun of his unusual stomach.

The result of all this was the world's first reliable explanation of the processes of digestion, a contribution which placed Dr. Beaumont among the immortals in the field of medicine. So thorough were Beaumont's methods that, although he labored under the difficulties of frontier fur-trading

Dr. William Beaumont collecting a specimen of gastric juice during his experiments on the stomach of Alexis St. Martin, a wounded Mackinac fur trader. This is a drawing of an oil painting by the American illustrator Dean Cornwell, and it is reproduced here by permission of John Wyeth & Brother, Inc., Philadelphia.

posts, doctors working in modern laboratories have been able to add but little to his discoveries. It is said that Dr. William Osler, the renowned medical authority, regarded Dr. Beaumont's work, and Harvey's discovery of the circulation of the blood, as the two foremost medical achievements of modern times. As for Alexis St. Martin, who served as a guinea pig for Dr. Beaumont's important experiments, he resumed strenuous work as a canoeman, farmer and wood-cutter; fathered a family of seventeen children, and lived to be eighty-three years old—outliving Dr. Beaumont by twenty-seven years. When he died, Dr. Osler offered his family a large sum of money for permission to do an autopsy and to place the famous stomach in the Army Medical Museum in Washington. But, poor as they were, the St. Martins refused; and in an effort to elude the doctors, they kept the body at home longer than usual. The weather was hot, and decomposition set in so badly that the dead man had to be left outside the church during his own funeral service. As a final precaution against any attempts to steal the stomach, the body was buried in a grave eight feet deep.

Henry Schoolcraft at Mackinac

During the year of the St. Martin accident—in 1822—Henry Schoolcraft came to the Mackinac country as government Indian agent, with headquarters at Sault Ste. Marie, and later at Mackinac Island. He held this position for nineteen years. Taking advantage of the rare opportunities offered by his work, Mr. Schoolcraft spent most of his leisure time in studying the thought, habits, language, customs, manners, folk-tales, religion, etc., of the Indians. In this he was aided by his wife, the grand-daughter of a prominent Ojibwa chief.

Henry Rowe Schoolcraft, government Indian agent at Sault Ste. Marie and Mackinac Island from 1822 to 1841, whose name—because of his many achievements as explorer, legislator, writer and Indian scholar—will always be closely associated with the early history of the Great Lakes region. This drawing is from a painting, and the signature is from the W. L. Clements Library.

And from the knowledge gained in this way, Mr. Schoolcraft prepared his extensive writings—including his six large volumes of "Archives of Aboriginal Knowledge," authorized by an act of Congress—on all aspects of Indian life. Many of the Indian myths and legends related in these writings are associated with Mackinac Island, which was a favorite camping-grounds and a sort of sacred shrine, or holy land, of the Ojibwa Indians. Here, the giant Indian demi-god, Manabozho, is said to have had his wigwam in the lofty rock called Sugar Loaf. Today, these works of Henry Schoolcraft are one of the most valuable sources of information on the Indian tribes of the United States. It was from them that the poet Longfellow obtained the raw material for his popular narrative poem, "The Song of Hiawatha," the scene of which is laid "in the land of the Ojibwas," near the Pictured Rocks of Upper Michigan.

The Mormon Kingdom of Michigan

Towards the close of the fur-trading days, when Mackinac was growing into a commercial fishing center, the region, for a time, became the home of a kingdom of Mormons, which, while it lasted, was the source of almost endless excitement and disturbance. In 1844, when an Illinois mob killed Joseph Smith, the founder of Mormonism, or the Church of Latter Day Saints, a clash for the right to succeed Smith as leader, took place between Brigham Young and James Strang. The latter was a New York lawyer of "erratic brilliance," who, in his youth, had written in his diary, "I am eager and mankind are frail . . . I shall act upon it for time to come for my own benefit." To fortify his claim as Smith's divinely-chosen successor, Strang dug up some metal hieroglyphic plates from under the roots of an oak tree, on

James Strang, whose activities as king of the Mormon colony on Beaver Island (1850-56), kept the inhabitants of Mackinac Island, and the neighboring region, in a perpetual state of turmoil and discord until he was assassinated by two of his followers. This drawing was made from a photograph of Strang in M. M. Quaife's book on the Beaver Island Mormons, "The Kingdom of Saint James." The autograph is from the Michigan Historical Collection.

White River, in Wisconsin. Although a follower of Strang later said that these plates were made from an old tea kettle, any doubts that they were "older than the Babylonian captivity of the Jews," or that they bore divine messages from heaven, were soon dispelled, in the minds of many, by Strang's exceptional gift for oratory and argument. By this means he managed to win over about two thousand members of the Church, whom he moved first to Voree (near Burlington), Wis., and later to Beaver Island, in Lake Michigan, about fifty miles from Mackinac Island; while Brigham Young led the rest across the country to Utah, where they founded Salt Lake City.

In those days, Beaver Island and Mackinac Island were linked together for judicial purposes; and from the moment that the Mormons appeared on Beaver Island the region was thrown into one prolonged period of turmoil and discord. This was caused by clashes between members of the Church and the non-Mormon inhabitants of Beaver Island, Mackinac-Island and the surrounding neighborhood. At first, the Mormons bore the abuses of the Beaver Island fishermen with comparative meekness; but as their numbers increased, and they became an important faction in the elections of Michigan—then closely contested—events took a turn in the opposite direction. By the spring of 1850, virtually all of Strang's colony had moved to Beaver Island; and on July 8th of that year, despite the efforts of the non-Mormons to prevent the affair with a *coup d'etat*, Strang had himself formally crowned King of the Mormon Church and state—"Apostle, Prophet, Seer, Revelator, and Translator of the Kingdom of God on Earth." During the coronation ceremonies, which were held in the half-finished log tabernacle, and attended by a crowd of about two thousand people, Strang wore a bright red robe, and his crown was "a plain metal circlet with a cluster of stars projecting in front."

The King's Five Wives

As absolute ruler of Beaver Island, Strang drew up his own laws and punishments, some of which were in conflict with the laws of the state and federal governments. Although he had previously declared that his strong opposition to polygamy, or "spiritual wifery," was "unchangeable," one glimpse of Elvira Field, a pretty 19-year-old school teacher and convert of his Church, caused the King to swerve a bit in his views on this question. Shortly, he received a "miraculous communication from heaven" to the effect that polygamy should be encouraged in the new kingdom; and he volunteered to set the example for his followers by taking Elvira as his second wife. In time, he collected a total of five wives, whose names were: Mary, Betsy, Sarah, Phoebe and of course, Elvira—all of whom deemed it an honor to be regarded as eligible to become a wife of the King. They bore him eleven children in about six years.

A Public Uproar

Although only about twenty of the five hundred families on Beaver Island became polygamous, such goings-on shocked Mackinac Island and the nearby mainland, whose inhabitants were thrown into an uproar. Soon, the Detroit, Cleveland and Buffalo newspapers were demanding the abdication of the King and the clean-up of Beaver Island. And all sorts of wild tales related that bands of Mormons were making night raids on neighboring towns to seize pretty maidens for the royal bed-chamber. President Fillmore, who happened to be in Detroit at the time visiting his brother, was given a lurid account of "disorder, riots, and crimes of the Mormon people at the Beaver Islands"; and he ordered a sweeping investigation, the story of which reads like a comic opera. Strang was charged with treason, robbery of the United States Mail, counterfeiting money, contempt of court, stealing timber from public lands, and a number of other odds and ends totaling twelve counts.

Mormon Colony Raided

To serve the warrants that were issued, the coast guard steamer "Michigan"—the first iron-clad vessel on the Great Lakes—dropped anchor at Mackinac Island, in June, 1851, where Judge Greig, the sole Mormon official of the county, was holding court—"sitting without his coat or cravat on the seat of justice . . . of the Kingdom of James the First." The ship's cannon were trained on the court-house building, half a musket shot away; and a party went ashore to arrest the judge, who, in turn, directed his aides to arrest the intruders for contempt of court. However, when told that resistance "would result in the destruction of the building and his own death," the judge surrendered and was taken on board the "Michigan."

Here he was told, "in the most solemn manner possible," that he would be hung from the yard-arm of the ship, "as certain as the stars twinkle above it," unless he informed the District Attorney, George C. Bates, how the King's house on Beaver Island could be located. Confronted by this outlandish threat, the judge inquired—pardonably enough—whether the District Attorney was drunk or just plain crazy. However, he at length gave out the information that was demanded—information that could have been easily obtained from any ordinary fisherman in the neighborhood. Arriving on Beaver Island in the middle of the night, the District Attorney and his "faithful deputy" entered Strang's house and quietly crept up stairs to the King's bedroom, where they found themselves in "a long, low room, where wide berths, heavily draped with stunning calico, shielded beds like the berths and staterooms of steamers, which proved to be occupied by Mormon women, four in a bed."

The Mormons in Court

Strang and a large number of his subjects were arrested and taken to Detroit for trial, where the courtroom was jammed for thirty days by a curious crowd, eager to hear shocking details of rampant sin on Beaver Island. One of the witnesses called was a Mrs. McCulloch, "a very sweet and accomplished lady from Baltimore, who had joined these people." On cross-examination she was asked: "Can it be possible that you are so blind as to really believe that that fellow who sits there beneath you—that Strang—is the prophet of the Lord, the successor to Him who bore his cross among the jeers and sneers of Mount Calvary?" To which she replied, while shaking her fist at her questioner: "Yes, you impudent District Attorney, and were you not a darned old fool, you would know it too." Strang conducting his own defense, made a dramatic speech to the jury in which he compared himself to Christ and the government lawyers to the Pharisees, who persecuted him; and so successful was he in his appeal that, in the end, despite the strong local feeling and the ceaseless newspaper attacks against the Mormons, Strang and his followers were freed of all charges.

The effect of all this was to increase Strang's prestige; and in 1853 he entered politics and was elected to the Michigan legislature, serving two terms. From this beginning, his political influence increased until he began to think of entering Congress; and even to dream of dictating, with his seven hundred Mormon votes, the issue of the approaching presidential election, which promised to be a close contest. He even felt strong enough to declare trade boycotts against Mackinac Island and Detroit; and to threaten Buffalo with similar measures if the residents of that city did not show a more friendly attitude towards the Mormons.

King Strang Assassinated

With the growth of his prestige and power, Strang developed into an inflexible ruler, adding more and more rules and regulations controlling the lives of his subjects. In time, resentment grew against his frequent infliction of "thirty lashes with a birch rod" for failure to live up to his decrees; and signs of a smoldering rebellion began to appear. One of Strang's numerous laws provided that his women subjects should clothe themselves in a short skirt with pantalet trousers. It is said that the Mormon women really liked this style of dress, but a few, at least, refused to wear the garment. One of the latter was Mrs. Thomas Bedford, whose husband encouraged her in her refusal, thereby incurring the condemnation of the King. Another of Strang's subjects, with whom he had come into conflict, was Alexander Wentworth, who is said to have been severely whipped for drinking. So Wentworth and Bedford, led by another malcontent, named Dr. McCulloch, began to plot Strang's downfall. On June 16, 1856,

Wentworth and Bedford, armed with horse pistols, hid behind some piles of cordwood on the Beaver Island dock; and as Strang approached to go on board the "Michigan," in response to a summons from the ship's captain, the two men arose and shot him three times. Although mortally wounded, Strang lived for three weeks, proving as hard to kill as Rasputin; and promptly after his death his Church and Kingdom died with him, his followers scattering in all directions. Notice was at once given by a mob to the Mormons that they must leave Beaver Island; and bands of ruffians shortly raided the colony, burning the tabernacle, looting the King's "palace," and driving the last members of the sect off the Island in a highly barbarous manner.

Today, on lonely Beaver Island, the village of St. James; the road called the King's Highway; Lake Galilee; and Jordan brook, remain to recall this unique American kingdom, which once flourished in the heart of Michigan, in the same district with Mackinac Island.

End of Fur Trading Days

As time went on, the merciless slaughter of the fur-bearing animals—with no one giving any thought to the future—soon wiped out some kinds of animals and made others almost equally rare. As a result, trade fell off, and Mackinac waned as a leading commercial center, a position it had held for almost two hundred years. In 1834, when the best fur-trading days had passed, John Jacob Astor retired from the business; and a number of years later (in 1854) the American

Fur Company left the Island. The local Indians, —whom the traders had induced to take to hunting as a business, instead of hunting, as they did originally, only to feed and clothe themselves—now became unemployed. Gradually they retreated to government reservations before the advancing tide of settlers, who were fast reducing the area of their hunting-grounds. Finally, to complete the decline of Mackinac, shortly before the turn of the century (in 1895), the United States government abandoned Fort Mackinac as a military post and turned it over to the State of Michigan. Long noted for its climate, natural beauty and historical associations, Mackinac then entered upon its present-day life as a popular resort for health seekers, vacationists and students of early American history.

THE MASSACRE OF OLD FORT MACKINAC, OR MICHILIMACKINAC

The Great Lakes Region in 1763

IN the spring of 1763, the region of the Great Lakes—as well as the greater part of the whole American continent—was an enormous stretch of wilderness. Most of the lands, east of the Mississippi River, were covered by dense forests of tall trees which had existed for unknown ages. This vast wilderness, teeming with natural wealth, and broken only here and there by winding water courses and Indian trails, was populated by a variety of wild animals, many of them bearing furs highly prized by white men. Yet, despite all its natural resources, the country served only as a mighty hunting-grounds and battlefield for a few wandering tribes of savage Indians, who lived in lodges, or tents, made of bark, over-lapping grass mats, or smoke-cured skins, stretched over a frame-work of poles.

These people, who were the first known race of men to inhabit America, were veritable wild men, whose general way of life was that of the Stone Age; and, before the coming of Europeans, they made their rude weapons and implements of bone, wood and stone. They lived as close to nature as the animals of the wilderness, whom they regarded as their equals; and their language abounded in picturesque expressions ladened with the odor of the lake, field and forest. Judged by modern American standards, their lives were not very comfortable; but since everyone among them lived the same, and since they were accustomed to hardship and exposure, they did not consider themselves unfortunate. Frequently there was little or nothing for them to eat, and when there was any, the food was poorly cooked and seasoned, and of little variety. They slept on mats, or on the bare ground, in their lodges,—which were often filled with blinding clouds of suffocating smoke—with the men, women, children and dogs all piling in in the most democratic fashion imaginable.

Although frequented by the French for more than a hundred years, the Great Lakes region was still almost entirely unsettled by white men. Jean Nicolet, the first white man to visit this part of the world, had paddled a birch-bark canoe through the Straits of Mackinac in 1634, while searching for the much-sought-after cross-country route to China; yet the only sign of a white settlement to be seen was a feeble fort and fur-trading post, garrisoned by a handful of soldiers and spotted here and there at key points along the watery highways. These posts were for controlling trade and travel, the latter being mainly by water, since roadways did not then exist. For the most part, no effort had been made by white men to take up permanent homes in the region; because their object up to that time was to preserve the western country as a perpetual hunting-grounds to supply the fur trade.

Description of Fort Michilimackinac

Three years before,—in 1760—as a result of the French and Indian War, the French had surrendered to their English rivals, the greater part of their vast claims in America, including the fort and trading post on the Straits of Mackinac. This settlement, known as Fort Michilimackinac, was a lonely outpost, buried in the depths of the northern wilderness. During the long, dreary winter it was ice-bound and cut off, like a hermitage, from communication with the main settle-

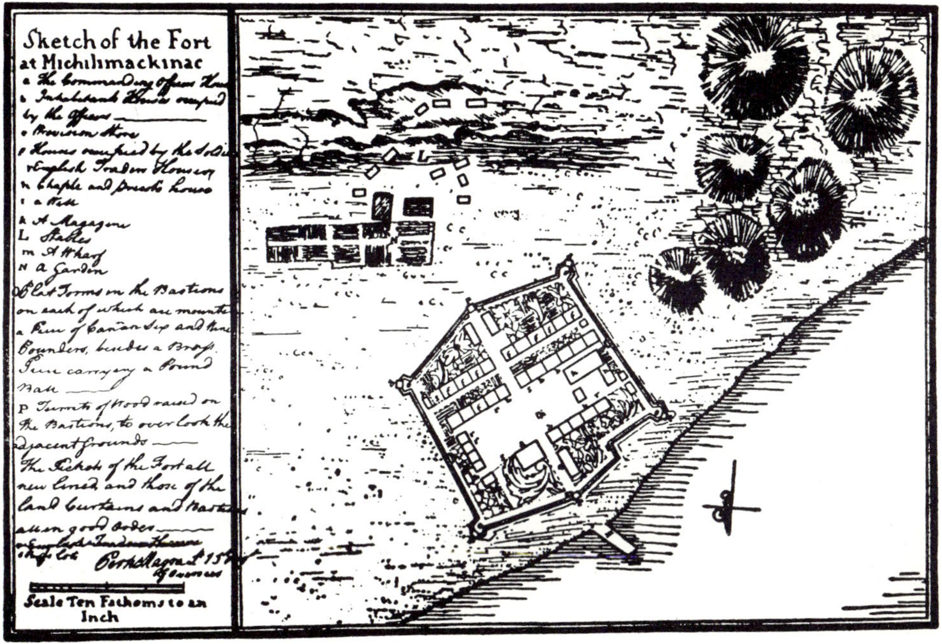

The Lieutenant Magra map of Fort Michilimackinac (about 1766) in the General Gage papers, W. L. Clements Library, upon which the centerpiece drawing of this book is based. The dark forms at the upper right represent sand hills.

ments at Montreal and Quebec. And frequently the inhabitants were long without word from the neighboring posts at Detroit, Sault Ste. Marie, Green Bay, Wis., and Fort St. Joseph, the latter standing near the present site of Niles, Michigan. The deadly monotony of life at the place, especially during the winter, made it an unpopular post among the soldiers. Fort Michilimackinac, at this time, stood on the southern shore of the Straits, within the present site of Mackinaw City, where the old stockade has been reconstructed. It was so close to the water's edge that when the wind was from the west the waves would break against the stockade.

Layout of Fort

Like Cadillac's little walled settlement of Fort Pontchartrain at Detroit, and other similar outposts in America at the time, Michilimackinac was not a fort in the sense that the term is commonly understood. It was, by no means, to be compared with the massive, well-equipped strongholds then in existence throughout the Old World. For it was intended only to afford protection against surprise attacks by the fickle and erratic Indians, whose arrows and musket balls could do no more than dent the stout cedar pickets. Nevertheless, the stockade or high fence of cedar poles, was laid out roughly along the lines of the big fortresses of those days, with bastions, or spear-shaped angles sticking out at the four corners. These were for use by the defenders of the fort in firing at the flanks of an attacking party trying to scale the walls of the stockade. On these bastions at Fort Michilimackinac there were two small brass cannon which the French had captured, a number of years before, from the British post on Hudson Bay.

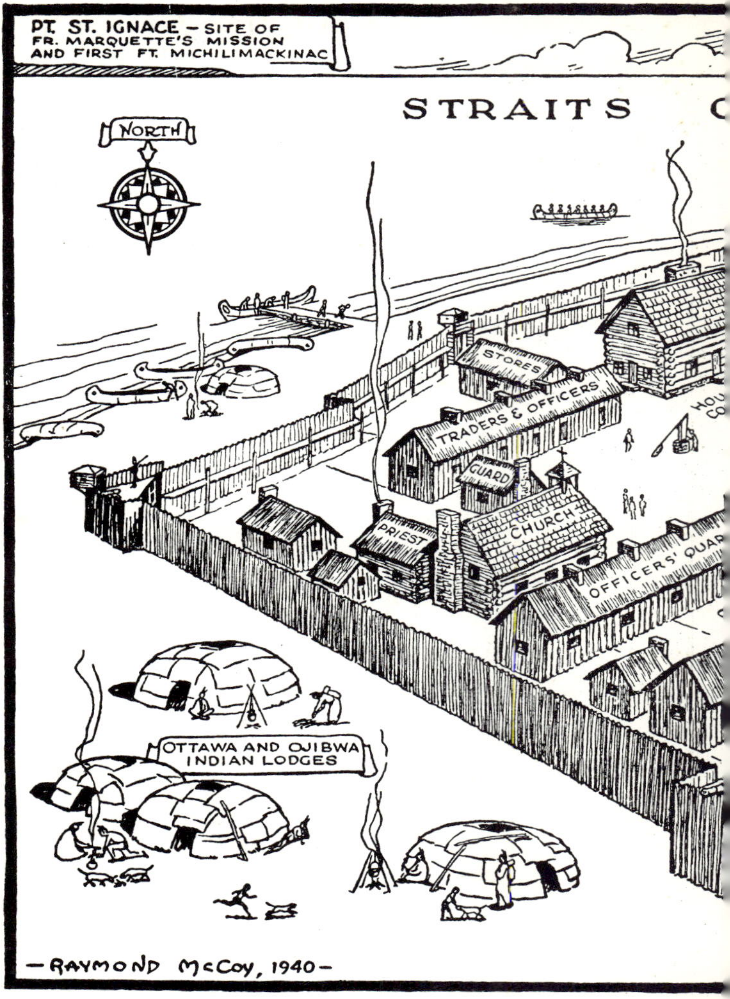

An imaginative drawing of Fort Michilimackinac (now Mackinaw C
map, and the descriptions of the fur trader, Alexander Henry, and
post,

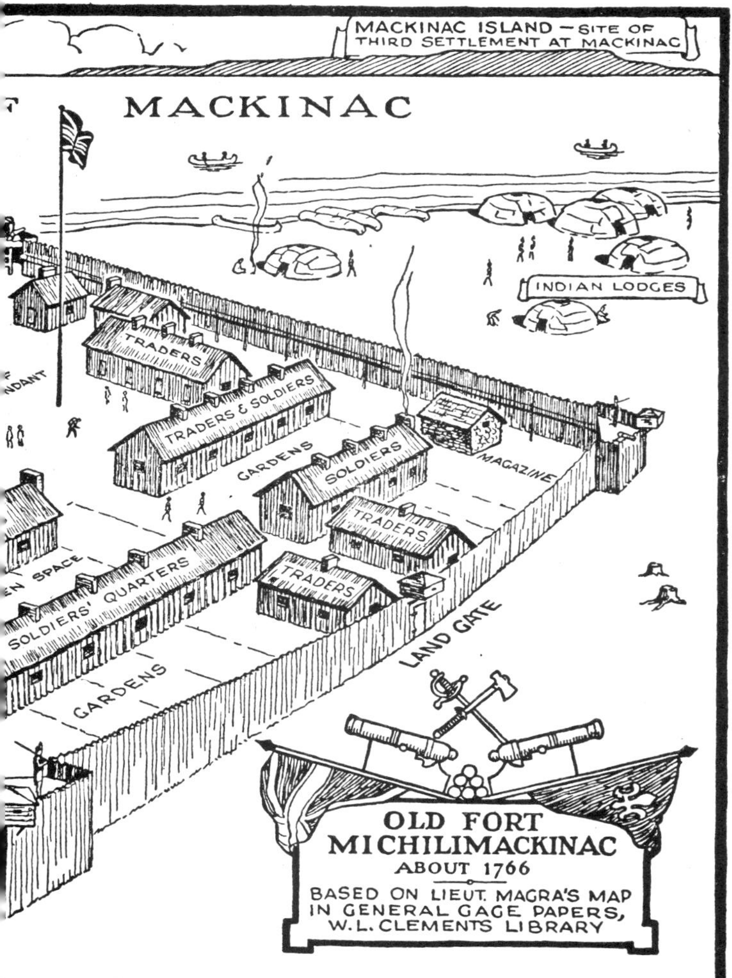

, about three years after the Indian massacre. Based on an authentic
British officer, Captain Beamsley Glazier, commandant of the
7-70.

The settlement proper of Michilimackinac was composed of a cluster of rude log buildings with bark roofs, including about thirty houses used by soldiers and traders. The soldiers' houses, according to Captain Beamsley Glazier, a former commandant, were made of "pickets set in the ground one storrie high, fill'd in with clay, and the roofs covered with bark, the chimneys made of clay and wood, all of which is so dry that I am obliged to have them swept twice a week, and to keep a large quantity of water in each room continually in case of fire." In addition to these soldiers' houses there was a Catholic church and priest's house, and a building or two for the storage of furs and articles used in trading with the Indians. These buildings formed a square around an open area, or common, and the whole—occupying about two acres—was enclosed within the stockade, something like a walled city of ancient times. The community was governed by the commandant and the laws in effect were those of the army, since arrangements for a civil government in the region had not yet been made.

The place served as a wilderness rendezvous for a picturesque assemblage of black-robed French Jesuit missionaries; half-savage Canadian fur traders; smartly-uniformed British soldiers; fierce-looking Indian warriors and gaudy-blanketed squaws with their unruly children of many hues. There were but few white women in the community, and some of the soldiers and fur traders had married among the Indians. Others did not concern themselves with the formality of a marriage ceremony. Money was not in use in the settlement, and the skins of beavers and other animals, were bartered for the goods of traders. Prices were sky-high, like those of an Alaskan boom town. Whitefish and trout—some of the latter weighing as much as sixty pounds—were caught in large numbers in the neighboring waters, which the Indians called the "Home of the Fishes." So fish, along with the dried meat of wild animals, Indian corn, maple sugar, some vegetables in the summer and an occasional supply of flour and pork from Montreal, served as the main articles of food. Indian and French-Canadian were the languages of the inhabitants, only a few of whom knew how to read and write.

The Fur Trade

In addition to its military value as a vantage point which guarded the gateway to the three upper Great Lakes, Fort Michilimackinac was a busy center of the fur trade. This trade was a great source of wealth—it was then Canada's chief means of support—and, at that time, it was the main reason for the presence of white men in the country. (While the first Frenchmen had been lured into the interior by the quest for new discoveries, the zeal for Christianizing the Indians, and the search for copper, silver, and other minerals, without the fur trade to attract them the Great Lakes region might have been left unexplored for ages.) Although carried on in a vast wilderness, where the law was but feebly enforced, this trade in furs was based entirely on a system of credit. The traders obtained their European-made Indian goods on credit from the Montreal merchants; and they in turn outfitted their employees, and issued goods on credit to the Indians. Despite the uncertainty of this arrangement, the parties concerned usually paid their debts.

The goods used for trading purposes were transported between Montreal and Michilimackinac over three different routes: by the Ottawa River, Lake Nipissing, French River and Georgian Bay;

An American beaver, with a beaver dam and lodge in the background. It was the skin of this animal—along with the skins of other fur-bearing animals—which served to attract the first white men into the Great Lakes region. This resulted in the exploration, and finally in the settlement, of the country by white men.

by Lake Ontario, Lake Simcoe and Georgian Bay; and by Lake Erie, the Detroit River and Lake Huron. Arriving at Michilimackinac with their merchandise, the traders hired their clerks (buyers) and canoemen, and each autumn sent out their canoes of trading goods to the regions of the Mississippi, Lake Michigan, Lake Superior and the Northwest. A part of these employees, or *engages*, as they were known, would spend a year, or more, trading for furs, in the distant Indian villages, and they were called *hivernants*, or winterers. The others, who were nicknamed *mangeurs de lard*, or pork-eaters,—"tenderfoots"—would return to Michilimackinac the next spring and summer, during the annual trading period, with their canoes grouped in picturesque flotillas, and freighted with heavy packs of furs, obtained by bartering goods to the Indians. Among these furs each year there were thousands of valuable skins of beavers, minks, muskrats, foxes, martins, otters, bears, etc., which, after the necessary bookkeeping had been completed, were loaded into other canoes and taken to Montreal; from where they were shipped to the markets of Paris, London, Vienna, and elsewhere.

How Beavers Were Hunted

While the skins of many animals were handled in trade, the fur of the beaver—then much in demand for beaver hats—was the most highly prized. To kill beavers, in those days, the Indians would go several miles up the rivers at dusk and let their canoes drift down with the current. At this time of the day the animals came out to obtain food or materials for their homes; and as the quiet approach of the canoes did not alarm them, the hunters were able to come within musket range. However, the most common method of taking beavers was to break open their houses with a tomahawk, or small axe, during the winter, when their fur was in its most valuable state. From their houses the animals would flee to their many washes, or holes, along the banks of the streams, and these the hunters located by tapping the ice for the hollow sound above the holes. Full holes were detected by the motion of the water above the entrances, caused by the breathing of the animals. The live animals were lifted out with the hands, and frequently the hunters received a nasty wound from the sharp teeth of the desperate beasts. Although they slaughtered beavers in great numbers for their skins, the French and Indian hunters never ceased to marvel at the intelligence and engineering skill of these animals, for whom they expressed greater admiration than for some human beings.

The beaver skins obtained in this way were sorted into various grades of quality; the most-prized grade being the cast-off skins which had been worn as clothing by the Indians until the skins had become soft and pliable by the grease from the bodies of the wearers. And many were the soft beaver skins, of this origin, which found their way into the expensive wardrobes of proud European nobles, who doubtless would have recoiled at the thought of accepting second-hand clothing from a humble savage of the American wilderness.

Birch-Bark Canoes

The canoes used on the long wilderness trading trips were a remarkable craft. They were patterned after the original birch-bark masterpieces of the Ojibwa, and other Algonquin tribes, which had been introduced long ago by some unknown savage inventor. They far exceeded in speed and lightness the clumsy, elm-bark canoes of the Iroquois tribes. and were perfectly adapted to the

Fur-traders in their birch-bark canoes passing over a wilderness stream on a trading expedition to the Indian hunting-grounds. This type of large trading canoe was known among the French-Canadian voyageurs, or canoemen, as a "canot du maitre," or master canoe. It was usually about forty feet long, and, in addition to the crew, it had a carrying capacity of about four tons.

shallow streams and many carrying places met with in wilderness travel.

Usually about forty feet long and about four feet wide in the middle, these canoes were made of strips of quarter-inch birch-bark, sewed together with spruce roots. They were strengthened with a framework of cedar ribs and cross-pieces, and made water-tight by pressing hot pitch into the seams. Their picturesque appearance was heightened by rude and showy designs painted on the gondola-shaped ends. Despite their strength, they were easily punctured, so a supply of roots, bark and pitch was always carried to repair frequent leaks caused by striking snags and stones.

Besides their crews of about eight husky men, these fragile and tipsy vessels could carry about four tons of goods and supplies—all of which had to be carefully balanced—and yet glide over the water with the buoyancy and stillness of a duck.

Other vessels used in the fur trade were small sailing ships and a long, low, flat-bottomed boat, pointed at both ends, called a *bateau*. This latter vessel was made of cedar wood and was propelled with oars and poles; and although it was more rugged than a canoe, it did not possess the same speed and lightness of this amazing craft.

The Fur-Trading Canoemen

The voyageurs, or canoemen, who handled these trading canoes, were—like the lumber-jacks of a later day—a singular class of men who existed only as long as the industry which gave them employment. Mostly French-Canadians, they were a light-hearted, half-wild band of men with flashing eyes and swarthy faces. No Englishman could match them in meeting the privations of wilderness trade, so they held a virtual monopoly of this

Voyageurs, or fur-trading canoemen, carrying their canoe and its cargo around a waterfall. Each of the crosses in the background was erected in memory of a canoeman who lost his life at this dangerous spot. This picture is from the book "The Voyageur," by Grace Lee Nute, illustrated by Carl W. Bertsch, and it is used here by permission of D. Appleton-Century Co., the publishers.

kind of employment. Like their Indian associates, whose superstitions and mode of life they had largely adopted, they were highly skilled in all the arts of life in the woods, and they felt out of place and hampered among the restraints of civilization. Dressed in their brightly-hued flannel and calico shirts, buck-skin trousers, tasseled and feathered stocking caps, gaudy sashes and rough shoes or moccasins, they were a strange blend of civilization and savagery. They could paddle briskly from dawn till dusk, while making the widerness resound with their gay boating songs, and take time out only for an occasional pipeful of tobacco. And for this strenuous labor, and the toils of carrying their canoes and heavy packs across the many portages from one waterway to another—some of them miles in length—they derived their amazing strength and endurance from a monotonous, but greatly relished, diet consisting of bear-fat, lyed-corn, dried peas, salt pork and an occasional wild animal or bird.

During the spring and summer,—the liveliest seasons of the community at Michilimackinac—these reckless fellows and their wood-ranging comrades, would swarm about the place in large numbers. Like a crew of sailors paid off after a long voyage, they would devote themselves to a spree of riotous living. And in a few weeks of feasting, drinking, dancing, fiddling and gambling, they would squander their entire earnings of the winter, then embark on another expedition into the wilds.

Feeling of Indians Towards British

Although the war between the French and the British was now over and the British had come into possession of the country, the Indian inhabitants were far from resigned to the outcome. The French had given up their claim,

Fur-trading canoemen repairing their damaged canoe in the wilderness While the man in the foreground uses a torch to soften the pitch over the seams, his comrade cuts a piece of bark from a pitch tree for use as a patch. This picture is from "The Voyageur," by Grace Lee Nute illustrated by Carl W. Bertsch, and it is used here by permission of D. Appleton-Century Co., the publishers.

but the Indians—who held a far older claim to the country—had no intentions of surrendering theirs. Not to the hated English, at any rate. Although unsteady in their loyalty, the tribesmen around the Great Lakes (except the Fox tribes of Wisconsin) had, for the most part, lived on good terms with the French. They had fought on their side during their long series of wars with the English—for possession of the Indians' lands—and they still adorned their war-dress with the scalp-locks of dead Englishmen.

An idea of the state of feeling which prevailed among the tribesmen, about this time, is to be gained from the experiences of the British traders who came to Fort Michilimackinac, in the late summer of 1761. Eager to begin trade with the Indians and enrich themselves with the fruits of victory, they hurried into the country before peace had been concluded and before British soldiers had arrived to take over the post. The French garrison, under Captain Beaujeu, had already departed, leaving the place in charge of the officer second in command, a native of Michilimackinac, the young half-breed, Lieutenant Charles de Langlade—one of the most remarkable men in the history of the old Northwest. (Trained for warfare literally from childhood, Langlade became a veteran leader of Indian war parties and, as an early settler of Green Bay, he is sometimes referred to as the "Father of Wisconsin." During his lifetime, it is said, he fought in ninety-nine battles and skirmishes. One of these encounters was an attack upon a British trading post in Ohio, in 1752, virtually the opening blow of the world-wide Seven Years' War. He also took part in the important battle on the Plains of Abraham, during the fall of Quebec, in 1759. He died in bed at the age of seventy-one, regretting that he had

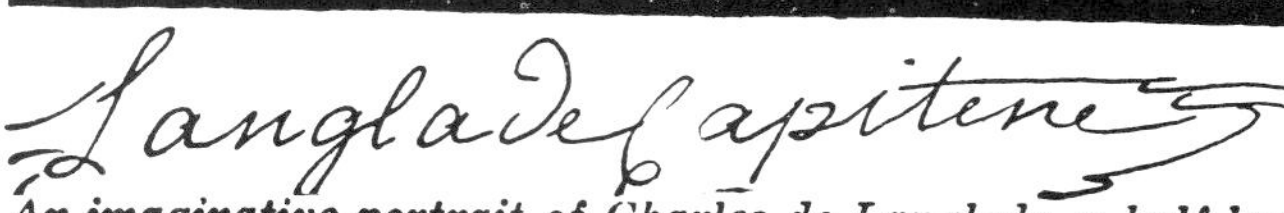

An imaginative portrait of Charles de Langlade, a half-breed fur trader and militiaman, born at Michilimackinac (Mackinaw City), in 1729, who is regarded as one of the most remarkable men in the early history of the Great Lakes region. He took part in numerous wilderness battles, and because of his prominence as an early settler of Green Bay, he is sometimes called the "Father of Wisconsin." One of the counties in that State today bears his name. The above autograph is from a Langlade letter owned by the Historical Society of Wisconsin.

been unable to battle once more and bring his total fights to one hundred.)

One of the adventurous traders who now came to Michilimackinac while Langlade was in charge, was the 22-year-old Alexander Henry, a native of New Jersey. He had journeyed from Montreal by the difficult old canoe route of the Ottawa River, Lake Nipissing, French River and Georgian Bay—the route by which Father Marquette and other early white men first ventured into Michigan. Henry had been warned several times on the way that the Indians were hostile to the English and that his life would be in great danger if he proceeded. And to preserve himself he resorted to the disguise of a Canadian canoeman. Arriving at Michilimackinac with his merchandise, he was coldly received by the jealous Canadian inhabitants, who discouraged the rival trader from remaining. They strongly urged him to flee to Detroit, where a garrison of British soldiers had been installed.

Visit of the Ojibwa Indians

But before he had time to consider the wisdom of this advice he received the disturbing news that the Ojibwa Indians (whom the English called Chippewas, through a misunderstanding of the French pronunciation), from Mackinac Island, were coming to call on him. A meeting followed, the details of which Henry relates in these words: "At two o'clock in the afternoon, the Chippewas came to the house, about sixty in number, and headed by Minavavana, their chief. They walked in single file, each with his tomahawk in one hand and scalping-knife in the other. Their bodies were naked from the waist upward, except in a few examples, where blankets were thrown loosely over the shoulders. Their faces were painted with charcoal, worked up with grease, their bodies with white clay, in patterns of various fancies. Some had feathers thrust through their noses, and their heads decorated with the same. It is unnecessary for me to dwell on the sensation with which I beheld the approach of this uncouth, if not frightful assemblage.

"Their chief entered first, and the rest followed without noise. On receiving a sign from the former, the latter seated themselves on the floor.

"Minavavana appeared to be about fifty years of age. He was six feet in height, and had in his countenance an indescribable mixture of good and evil. Looking steadfastly at me, where I sat in ceremony, with an interpreter on either hand, and several Canadians behind me, he entered at the same time, into conversation with Campion [Henry's Canadian assistant], inquiring how long it was since I left Montreal, and observing that the English, as it would seem, were brave men, and not afraid of death, since they dared to come, as I had done, fearlessly among their enemies.

"The Indians now gravely smoked their pipes, while I inwardly endured the tortures of suspense. At length the pipes being finished, as well as a long pause, by which they were succeeded, Minavavana, taking a few strings of wampum in his hand, began the following speech:

Chief Minavavana Addresses Henry

" 'Englishman, it is to you that I speak, and I demand your attention. Englishman, you know that the French king is our father. He promised to be such; and we, in return promised to be his children. This promise we have kept. Englishman, it is you that have made war with this our father. You are his enemy; and how then could you have the boldness to venture among us, his children? You know that his enemies are ours. Englishman, we are informed that our father, the King of France, is old and infirm; and that, being fatigued with making war upon your nation, he is fallen asleep. During his sleep, you have taken advantage of him, and possessed yourselves of Canada. But his nap is almost at an end. I think I hear him already stirring, and inquiring for his children, the Indians; and when he does awake, what must become of you? He will destroy you utterly.

"'Englishman, although you have conquered the French, you have not yet conquered us. We are not your slaves. These lakes, these woods and mountains were left to us by our ancestors. They are our inheritance; and we will part with them to none. Your nation supposes that we, like the white people, cannot live without bread and pork and beer. But you ought to know that He, the Great Spirit and Master of Life, has provided food for us in these spacious lakes, and on these woody mountains.

"'Englishman, our Father, the King of France, employed our young men to make war upon your nation. In this warfare, many of them have been killed; and it is our custom to retaliate until such time as the spirits of the slain are satisfied. But the spirits of the slain are to be satisfied in either of two ways; the first is by the spilling of the blood of the nation by which they fell; the other, by covering the bodies of the dead and thus allaying the resentment of their relations. This is done by making presents.

"'Englishman, your king has never sent us any presents, nor entered into any treaty with us; wherefore he and we are still at war; and, until he does these things, we must consider that we have no other father nor friend, among the white men, than the King of France; but for you, we have taken into consideration that you have ventured your life among us in the expectation that we should not molest you. You do not come armed, with the intention to make war; you come in peace to trade with us, and supply us with necessaries, of which we are in much want. We shall regard you, therefore, as a brother; and you sleep tranquilly, without fear of the Chippewas. As a token of friendship, we present you this pipe to smoke.'

"As Minavavana uttered these words, an Indian presented me with a pipe, which, after I had drawn the smoke three times, was carried to the chief, and after him to every person in the room. This ceremony ended, the chief arose and gave me his hand, in which he was followed by all the rest."

To this speech, Henry replied, by means of an interpreter, with corresponding expressions of friendship, after which the Indians requested that he give them some rum, or "English milk" as they called it; for, they said, they wished to compare its taste with that of French brandy. Fearfully, —for he knew what a dangerous combination a drunken Indian and his weapons can be—the trader distributed a small quantity among them, along with some presents of beads, knives, tobacco, etc.; and the savages departed in apparent good humor. But he had scarcely finished his sigh of relief at getting rid of these unwelcome guests when danger threatened from another quarter.

Visit of Ottawa Indians

About twenty miles southwest of the fort, along the shore of Lake Michigan, somewhere between the present Cross Village and Harbor Springs, stood the Indian village of L'Arbre Croche, or Crooked Tree, where the Ottawa Indians boasted of two hundred and fifty fighting men. (Several Ottawa and Ojibwa Indian families still live in this neighborhood at the present time.) Here about 1742, the French Jesuits had rebuilt the mission of St. Ignace, which Father Marquette had originally established on the present site of St. Ignace. This mission was now in charge of Father Pierre Du Jaunay. The Ottawa of L'Arbre Croche —unlike the Ojibwa Indians, who were still utter savages—were somewhat improved from their original savage state, growing enough corn, beans and pumpkins for themselves and the inhabitants of Fort Michilimackinac. A party of these Indians now came to the fort and summoned Henry and two other traders, named Stanley Goddard and Ezekiel Solomon, to meet them in council at the commandant's house.

At this meeting the Ottawa made the startling demand that the traders distribute all their merchandise among their men on credit, offering in return only a meaningless promise to pay with their beaver-skins when they returned from their hunting-grounds the following summer. A refusal, the traders were told, meant death, and they were given until morning to make up their minds. Realizing that compliance with the demand meant financial ruin, Henry and his companions resolved upon resistance. They armed about thirty of their men with muskets and barricaded themselves in Henry's cabin within the fort. A strict watch was kept all night, but the Ottawa did not venture an attack. The next day the Canadian inhabitants, still hopeful of getting rid of their English competitors, advised them to surrender; but they stubbornly held their ground, and towards evening they received the joyful news that a detachment of British troops, on their way to garrison the fort, were encamped only a few miles away. Another nerve-racking night of watching ensued, for much might happen before morning. However, at daybreak, the Ottawa, unsuccessful in their efforts to enlist the support of the Canadians in a proposed attack upon the advancing soldiers, launched their canoes and returned to L'Arbre Croche.

Arrival of British Garrison

The next day, September 28, 1761, Captain Henry Balfour, of the 80th Regiment, or Gage's Light Infantry, and a detachment of red-coated British troops marched into the fort. Langlade surrendered the post, and the flag of the old British Union was raised to the top of the flagstaff. Balfour called a council with the Indian chiefs; obtained their consent for the British to remain in the country and, leaving Lieutenant William Leslie and twenty-eight men to garrison Michilimackinac, he journeyed on with the rest of his troops to occupy the forts of Sault Ste. Marie, Green Bay and St. Joseph (Niles).

Indian Discontent

Months passed, and while the Indians maintained an outward appearance of friendship, their hostility towards the British did not diminish. They found a big difference between the jovial, easy-going French soldiers and traders, and the cool and reserved British. For the French treated them with tact and respected their peculiar customs and superstitions, while the British looked upon them with contempt and complained roughly about the trouble they caused in hanging around the fort.

To add to their resentment, the English failed to observe the practice introduced by the French of making "presents" to them, from time to time, of blankets, muskets, hatchets, knives, powder, shot, tobacco, kettles, etc. This the French had done to retain the friendship and good will of the tribesmen. The articles thus received the Indians, originally, either made themselves or

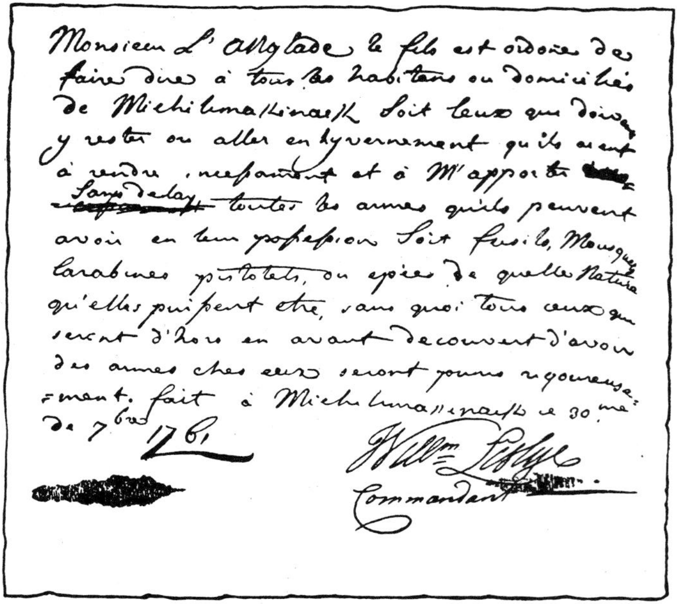

Monsieur L'Anglade le fils est ordonné de
faire dire à tous les habitans ou domiciliés
de Michilimakinack soit ceux qui doivent
y rester ou aller en hyvernement qu'ils aient
à rendre incessamment et à M'apporter
Sans delay toutes les armes qu'ils peuvent
avoir en leur possession soit fusils, Mousquets
carabines pistolets, ou epées de quelle Nature
qu'elles puissent etre, sans quoi tous ceux qui
seront d'hors en avant decouvert d'avoir
des armes chez eux seront punis rigoureuse-
-ment. fait à Michilimakinack le 30.me
de 7bre 1761

Willm Leslye
Commandant

This is one of the first orders issued by a British officer after the British took over Fort Michilimackinac from the French, on September 28, 1761, following the close of the French and Indian War. Dated two days after the arrival of the British, the order is signed by Lieutenant William Leslye (also spelled Leslie, Lesley and Lessley), the new commandant, and it is addressed to Charles de Langlade, the former commandant and the leading Frenchman of the community. The document is written in French and a translation of it reads: "Monsieur Langlade, the son [that is, Charles de Langlade, the son of Augustin de Langlade], is ordered to notify all the inhabitants residing at Michilimackinack, whether they live there or are only spending the winter there, that they are to bring to me, without delay, all the arms which they have in their possession, whether they be rifles, muskets, carbines, pistols, or swords of any nature; and all those discovered with arms from now on will be punished rigorously. Made at Michilimackinack the 30th of September, 1761. William Leslye, Commandant." The original manuscript is in the Edward E. Ayer Collection, of the Newberry Library, Chicago.

managed to get along without. But during the long period of French control they became accustomed to these luxuries and were no longer satisfied with their own bows and arrows, stone axes and other articles. As a matter of fact, in adopting the equipment of white men, they soon lost the art of making and using their own rude weapons and implements. Hence, they became unable to feed and clothe themselves without the articles that were presented to them by government agents, or bartered to them by traders in exchange for their furs; so when the British suddenly withheld their goods, much want and suffering resulted among the tribesmen.

To complicate matters further, the British fur traders were not as considerate or as well managed as those of the French. Under the more liberal British trading regulations, permits to trade were issued to everyone who wanted them; and the woods swarmed with competing traders—some of them "rugged individualists" of the most ruthless variety. The pressure of competition was tremendous; and in a region where law meant but little, the traders fought among themselves and cheated and plundered the unsophisticated Indians; under-weighing their furs, over-charging for goods and trading them liquor highly diluted with water.

The Gathering Storm

The French inhabitants of the conquered region had taken the oath of allegiance to England, but they still spoke French and retained their French customs and sympathies. They saw the possibilities that the situation offered for revenge on their conquerors and competitors in the fur trade, and with lies and false encouragements of French aid, incited the tribesmen to an outbreak which was not long in coming. As early as the summer of

1761, Captain Campbell, the commandant at Detroit, had discovered a plot to destroy him and his men, along with the British garrisons of several other posts. And other schemes of a like nature were detected and quickly nipped in the bud. However, the English were treating symptoms and overlooking causes. Their alertness postponed the gathering storm, but could not prevent it entirely.

Uprising of Chief Pontiac

In the spring of 1763, with the stage thus set for an uprising, a scheme was matured which the master historian, Francis Parkman, has referred to as "greater in extent, deeper and more comprehensive in design—such a one as was never before or since conceived or executed by a North American Indian." It was the product of a middle-aged Ottawa chief named Pontiac, whose proud nature burned with bitter resentment because the British had not given him the same respectful treatment that he had received from the French.

Pontiac is described as a man of medium height; of strong, muscular build, and of such exceptional ability and character that he occupied a position of distinction not only among his own people, but among the neighboring tribes as well. He is regarded as one of the ablest Indians produced in North America. Yet with all his good qualities, he was still basically a savage. Like his fellowmen, and the great Chief Tecumseh of a later day, he was convinced that civilization is inferior to savagery, because it restricts too much the freedom of the individual; and, to use a modern argument, is thus "un-American." Pontiac's home was on Peche Island, just east of Belle Isle, near Detroit. A number of years before, he had led the Ottawa Indians in turn-

An imaginative portrait of the Ottawa Indian chief, Pontiac, who organized and directed the Indian uprising in the spring of 1763, of which the massacre of Fort Michilimackinac was a part. This picture is based on a drawing by the late J. L. Kraemer, in The Detroit News. The crude figure of an animal beneath it is said to be Pontiac's mark. It is supposed to be the figure of an otter, which was Pontiac's totem, or clan emblem. These totems were used by the Indians to sign their names.

ing back an attack on the French garrison at Detroit by the hostile Fox Indians. And it is believed that he was also present in the war party, led by Charles de Langlade, when the British, under General Braddock,—aided by the 23-year-old George Washington—were routed near the present site of Pittsburgh, in 1755.

Pontiac's War Plan

Pontiac's scheme was to attack the British forts, all about the same time, and thus prevent them from sending one another assistance. Then with the soldiers wiped out, the Indians would turn upon the defenseless settlers, destroy them and their homes, and reclaim the lands which had been taken over by the white men. As someone has aptly said, this was probably the first of our many "America - for - the - one - hundred - percent - Americans" campaigns.

The size and difficulty of such an undertaking is better appreciated when we consider the peculiar character of the Indians. Their strong individual nature made them as unruly as the winds and the poorest kind of material for building an army with any sort of discipline. To add to the problem, the Indians had no laws, either civil or military. They had ancient customs and traditions which took the place of laws and thus maintained order in their communities; but these customs and traditions offered no established means of providing strong leadership in times of emergency. (Surely, this was freedom with a vengeance!) Hence, when Indian warriors acted in large numbers they were usually as flighty and unsystematic as a mob of children. It was only in small war parties, inspired by the hope of taking a few scalps, that they were at their best as fighting men.

The task which lay before Pontiac may then be imagined. Under the very loose Indian system of government, the only authority he possessed—the only means he had of inducing his followers to obey his commands—was derived from the respect the Indians held for his reputation as a warrior and his natural ability as a leader. And while hero-worship had an important influence on Indian behavior, it was only a man like Pontiac who could depend on this influence to execute a large-scale military operation, such as he had in mind.

To complete arrangements for carrying out his design, Pontiac held a great war council, towards the close of April, on the banks of the Ecorse River, not far from Detroit. At this council he resorted to every device of his unusual oratorial ability to arouse the blood-thirsty spirit of the assembled chiefs and to move them to join in his plot. He denounced the English for their greed, snobbishness and injustice. He contrasted them with the more agreeable French; pointed out the grave peril of their land-grabbing policies and urged his savage listeners to rise up, drive the invader from the soil of their forefathers and ward off the threatening doom of their race.

Indian Mode of Warfare

Pontiac's appeal had the desired effect, and all resolved to take up the hatchet and join in the fray. It is unlikely that details of the assaults upon the various posts were discussed at this time, but everyone knew that no attacks were to be undertaken in the open. For the Indian method of warfare differed greatly from that of the white men of their time. Because of their extreme caution, their style of fighting consisted mainly of swift raids and skirmishes in which the enemy was subjected to ambush, treachery, or otherwise taken by surprise. For in their view, trickery was wisdom, and to attack in the open in stand-up-and-fight fashion was sheer foolishness, not bravery. Their constant aim was to fight only under an advantage, and thus to inflict injury without suffering loss themselves. To achieve this end no holds were barred. This was not necessarily because the Indians were cowards. They were savages and their point of view was something like that of children. When the occasion required it, they could be among the bravest of the brave. They could endure being tortured and burned alive with an unflinching calmness, or scornful defiance, that made white men marvel at their fortitude.

During the winter of 1762-63, Pontiac's messengers made their way through the snow-covered forests, to distant Indian villages, in every direction; carrying a war-belt of black and purple wampum, and a tomahawk painted red, as a symbolic invitation to the various tribes to take part in the coming war. The blow was to be struck during the month of May, the exact time being set by the phases of the moon, which—along with the rising and setting of the sun, and the physical changes of the seasons—was the usual means by which the Indians designated points in time.

Indian War Begins

Pontiac, himself, assumed charge of the attack upon the important post of Detroit; and when his treacherous plot was defeated by the previous warning of the commandant, he opened seige of the fort there on May 9th. By the 27th, Fort Sandusky (in Ohio), Fort St. Joseph (near Niles), and Fort Miami (Fort Wayne, Ind.) had been taken and their garrisons captured or slaughtered. Soor Fort Ouiatanon (near the present Lafayette, Ind.) Fort Presque Isle (now Erie, Pa.), and Fort

Chief Pontiac and Major Gladwin, British commandant at Detroit, in 1763, at the meeting requested by Pontiac with the intention of making a surprise attack upon the garrison of the fort. Gladwin had been warned in advance of the plans of the Indians and he had his soldiers fully armed for the occasion. Pontiac and his men (with knives, tomahawks and filed-off muskets under their blankets) accordingly went away to begin a five-month siege of Detroit two days later, on May 9, 1763. This picture is from a mural painting by Gari Melchers in the Detroit Public Library. It is reproduced here through the courtesy of the Edison Institute. Dearborn. Mich.

LeBoeuf and Venango, in northwestern Pennsylvania, were to fall victims of various forms of treachery; while Fort Pitt (Pittsburgh), Fort Niagara (at the mouth of the Niagara River), and Forts Ligonier and Bedford, in southwestern Pennsylvania, as well as the borders of the eastern settlements, were to be centers of bloodshed and devastation. The whole country was afire with Indian warfare.

Along with the other tribes, the Indians around the Straits of Mackinac had agreed to join in the crusade; and when, about the end of May, the Ojibwa received word that the fighting had begun at Detroit, their native appetite for blood and glory was stirred to a high pitch of excitement. They began at once to arrange for the attack upon Fort Michilimackinac. However, as the result either of jealousy or suspicion of the northern Ottawa Indians,—who were known to be quite friendly with the English—or a desire to keep all the glory and plunder for themselves, the Ojibwa determined to make the assault without notifying their friends and neighbors at L'Arbre Croche.

Size of the Fort Garrison

Fort Michilimackinac, at this time, was again becoming a busy center of the fur trade, following the interruption in trade caused by the recent French and Indian War. Things generally were about the same as when trader Henry and the British troops arrived in the fall of 1761, except that Captain George Etherington was now the commandant. According to a report of this officer, the garrison now consisted of himself, Lieutenants William Leslie and John Jamet and thirty-five privates. All were members of the 60th Regiment, known as the Royal Americans, a regiment which had fought under General Wolfe

The Great Lakes Region
SHOWING THE EXTENT OF THE CHIEF PONTIAC WAR AND ALSO THE LOCATION OF MANY OF THE PLACES REFERRED TO IN THIS BOOK
50 MI 100 MI
DISTANCE SCALE
N
TO LAKE OF THE WOODS AND THE NORTHWEST
PORT ARTHUR
FT WILLIAM
GRAND PORTAGE
ISLE ROYAL
MINNESOTA
Lake Superior
DULUTH
ASHLAND SITE OF THE INDIAN MISSION OF LAPOINTE DE ST ESPRIT
S S MARIE SITE OF AN INDIAN MISSION BEGUN BY FR MARQUETTE IN 1668
MICHILIMACKINAC
ST IGNACE
BEAVER I
FORT MICHILIMACKINAC TAKEN BY THE INDIANS ON JUNE 2, 1763
MICHIGAN
WISCONSIN
GREEN BAY FROM THIS PLACE LIEUT GORRELL WENT TO THE AID OF MICHILIMACKINAC IN 1763
Lake Michigan
Lake Huron
Saginaw Bay
Georgian Bay
L NIPISSING
FRENCH R
OTTAWA RIVER
THE OTTAWA RIVER-GEORGIAN BAY ROUTE WAS USED BY EARLY CANOE TRAVELERS FOR MANY YEARS IN JOURNEYING BETWEEN MONTREAL AND THE GREAT LAKES
MONTREAL
CANADA
LAKE SIMCOE
KINGSTON
ST LAWRENCE RIVER
LAKE CHAMPLAIN
VERMONT
FORT TICONDEROGA
LAKE GEORGE
FORT WILLIAM HENRY
ALBANY
HUDSON RIVER
MASS
CONN
NEW YORK
NEW JERSEY
NEW YORK CITY
PULASKI
Lake Ontario
FORT NIAGARA NEAR THE SCENE OF THE MASSACRE OF DEVILS HOLE IN 1763
NIAGARA RIVER
Lake Erie
ERIE
FORTS PRESQUE ISLE ① LE BOEUF ② AND VENANGO ③ ALL OF WHICH WERE TAKEN BY THE INDIANS IN 1763
PENNSYLVANIA
PITTSBURGH
FORTS PITT ④ LIGONIER ⑤ AND BEDFORD ⑥ WHICH WERE ATTACKED BY THE INDIANS IN 1763 BUT WERE NOT CAPTURED
DETROIT SITE OF CADILLAC'S FORT PONTCHARTRAIN BESIEGED BY CHIEF PONTIAC FOR FIVE MONTHS IN 1763
LAKE ST CLAIR
DETROIT RIVER
NILES—SITE OF FORT ST JOSEPH TAKEN BY THE INDIANS IN 1763
SANDUSKY SITE OF A FORT TAKEN BY THE INDIANS IN 1763
OHIO
FT WAYNE—SITE OF FORT MIAMI TAKEN BY INDIANS IN 1763
INDIANA
LAFAYETTE—SITE OF FT OUIATANON TAKEN BY INDIANS IN 1763
CHICAGO SITE OF THE FORT DEARBORN INDIAN MASSACRE IN 1812
ILLINOIS
IOWA
MISSISSIPPI
RIVER
WISCONSIN RIVER
PRAIRIE DU CHIEN WHERE MARQUETTE AND JOLLIET FIRST SAW THE MISSISSIPPI RIVER
R McCoy

at Quebec. Lieutenant Jamet and his small detachment had been added to the garrison during the previous winter when their original post, at Sault Ste. Marie, was accidentally destroyed by fire. Four British traders—Tracy, Henry, Bostwick and Solomon—and three hundred Canadians completed the number of inhabitants of the settlement.

Indians Assemble for Attack

The number of Indians in the neighborhood had lately been more than doubled by the arrival of several bands of wandering tribes, attracted probably by whispered words of the impending storm. Encamped in the neighboring woods were a large number of Ojibwa Indians recently arrived; while several bands of Sauk Indians (from whose name Saginaw is derived), from the River Wisconsin, had also erected their lodges in the vicinity. Altogether, the savage population was now about four hundred. But, strangely enough, these unusual numbers excited no serious alarm among the members of the garrison. Probably this was partly because the British felt secure in their fort against the Indians, whose only weapons were muskets, knives, clubs and tomahawks; and partly because the behavior of the Indians was so erratic that a certain amount of irregularity was taken for granted. The tribesmen were now frequenting the fort, as was customary, trading the furs taken during their winter's hunt; loafing about with an air of calm unconcern, and begging for tobacco, gunpowder and liquor.

Now and then some trader coming to the fort from the nearby Indian encampment would report that the behavior of the savages made him suspect that something mischievous was in the air; or "some scoundrel half-breed would be heard boasting in his cups that before next summer he would have English hair to fringe his hunting frock."

Advance Warning

On one occasion Laurent Ducharme, a friendly Canadian, distinctly told Captain Etherington that a definite plan had been arranged for destroying him and his garrison, and all the English in the Great Lakes region. Charles de Langlade also warned Etherington that he should prepare for trouble. But the commandant—like General Braddock, and some of the other British officers who under-rated the Indians—turned a deaf ear to the warning. He strongly berated Ducharme for reporting what he regarded as nothing more than a mischievous rumor, and threatened to send, as a prisoner to Detroit, the next person who should disturb the community with such unwelcome tidings.

Alexander Henry, the trader, likewise distrusted the Indians; but upon his suggesting to the commandant that he be on his guard, Etherington responded with laughter and ridiculed the trader for his timidity. However, Henry, the adviser in this instance, was himself, as he confesses, later also guilty of disregarding a similar warning, although under somewhat different circumstances.

Wawatam's Friendship With Henry

At the close of May, Henry was visited by an Ojibwa chief named Wawatam. This Indian was a kindly man, about forty-five years of age, who had become strongly attached to Henry in a manner peculiar to a custom of the Indians. The previous year, at the time of their first meeting, Wawatam had entered the trader's house with a large present of furs, sugar, and dried meat. Lay-ing these on the floor, he began a speech, informing Henry that early in life (when he was about fourteen years old), according to an ancient custom of his people, he had withdrawn to a place of solitude to fast and pray in an effort to enlist the protection and guidance of the Great Spirit during his lifetime.

In the course of dreams and visions which Wawatam experienced on this occasion, it was revealed to him that, later in life, he would meet a white man whom he should adopt as a son, friend, and brother. His first glimpse of young Henry had convinced him that he was the man whom his guiding spirit had in mind and that his dream was now fulfilled.

Prompted merely by a desire to be agreeable, Henry accepted the present, and replied that he would be pleased to have so good a man as Wawatam appeared to be, for a friend and brother. He made a present in return, and as he shortly afterwards left for a stay at Sault Ste. Marie, memory of the incident soon left his mind.

Many months had passed since this happening, and on the last day of May, Wawatam again visited Henry. He had just returned from his winter's hunt and appeared to be much depressed and deeply absorbed in thought. Henry inquired about his health, but without replying, Wawatam expressed surprise and regret at finding the trader at Michilimackinac, being under the impression that Henry was still at Sault Ste. Marie. Wawatam said that he was himself going to the Sault the following morning and that he wished the trader to accompany him and his family.

Wawatam's Warning

Wawatam then inquired whether the commandant had heard any bad news; and he mentioned that while wintering he had been often troubled by "the noise of evil birds." He pointed out that there was an abnormally large number of Indians encamped near the fort, many of whom had avoided showing themselves within the stockade. But unable to make Henry understand the hints he gave him, Wawatam at length went away, wearing a sad and mournful look. Early the next morning, he appeared again; this time accompanied by his squaw, who brought a present of dried meat. He again begged Henry to go with him to the Sault, explaining that the Indians were coming the next day to ask for liquor and that he might be killed after they became intoxicated. Wawatam resorted to many suggestions and pleadings to draw Henry away from Fort Michilimackinac without at the same time betraying the plot and thus exposing himself and his family to the rage of his fellowmen. But due to Henry's limited knowledge of the Indian language,—with its extravagantly figurative expressions and numerous ways of saying the same thing—the trader did not understand the warning that was given him. Although suspicious of the Indians himself, he says that "nothing induced me to believe that serious mischief was at hand." He therefore explained to Wawatam that he could not leave Michilimackinac until his clerks had returned from their winter's trading expedition. So disappointed with the failure of their appeals, Wawatam and his squaw departed in tears.

Preparations for Attack

During the same day, Henry observed that the fort was crowded with Indians, moving about restlessly, but with every appearance of friendship; for although intensely excitable by nature, the tribesmen were masters at concealing their thoughts and emotions. Some of them came to Henry's house to buy tomahawks, often asking him to show them silver arm-bands and other ornaments, with no other intention, as it afterwards developed, than to learn where they were kept, in order that they might find them readily at the moment of pillage. The day closed peacefully and many of the doomed English garrison watched for the last time the sunset glow as it lingered over the waters of Lake Michigan.

The Indian Ball Game

The following morning was the second of June. (This date is confirmed by all reports written at the time. The date of June fourth is supported only by trader Henry's account, which was written —partly from memory—in 1809, forty-six years after the massacre took place.) The weather was sultry, and the waves lapped quietly on the nearby shore. Since their arrival from their winter's hunt, the Indians had been entertaining themselves, almost every day, by playing ball; and on this day a big game was to be played between the Sauk and the Ojibwa Indians for a high wager. A mixed multitude of Canadians, plumed and painted Indian chiefs, naked warriors and blanketed squaws thronged the open ground outside the south, or land, gate of the fort, to witness, and to take part in, the contest. Captain Etherington and Lieutenant Leslie stood just outside the gate, the commandant having promised the Ojibwa that he would place a bet on them to defeat the Sauk.

The game which the Indians played on this memorable occasion was ideally suited to the purpost at hand—to divert the attention of the garrison. Among the Ojibwa it was known as *baggattaway*, and it was long a favorite sport among many Indian tribes. The Canadians called it *le jeu de la crosse*, and it was in this way that its modern name of lacrosse was derived.

Indians playing baggattaway, a game which has been adopted by white ***men from the Indians under the name of lacrosse. This is the game the Indians played outside the south, or land gate, of Fort Michilimackinac (Mackinaw City), on June 2, 1763, in order to make a surprise attack upon the fort and to massacre the British inhabitants.***

It was played with a long-handled racket, and a wooden ball, the former consisting of a stick curved at one end and woven loosely with rawhide to form a kind of net. In this the ball was caught and hurled, or carried, about the field. At both ends of the field a tall post was planted, marking the goals of the opposing teams. The object of each side was to drive the ball to the goal of its opponents and to defend its own territory from invasion. Several hundred savage athletes often thronged the playing field in a single game; leaping, sprinting, yelping, colliding and struggling with their adversaries in a wild pursuit of the elusive ball. Adding to the distraction and confusion of the game was the laughter and cheering of the spectators, whose shouts of excitement and applause filled the air with a noisy tumult.

The Attack and Massacre

At about noon, when the contest, on this second day of June, was at its height, the ball suddenly rose, as if by accident, from the tangle of struggling forms; soared through the air and fell close to the open gate of the stockade. At once, hundreds of frenzied Indians, their dark, bead-like eyes flashing fiercely, dashed towards the gate, like a pack of hounds in full cry; apparently in hot pursuit of the ball. Every move was so well carried out that the soldiers of the fort failed to detect that this seemingly chance stroke was the signal for the beginning of a well-planned assault. The mask of friendship was immediately dropped; the cheering changed to a war-whoop; and the unsuspecting English were completely overwhelmed. The squaws deftly passed to the sprinting warriors the knives and tomahawks concealed beneath their blankets for the occasion. And the blood-shed began. Captain Etherington and Lieutenant Leslie were quickly overpowered from behind by swarthy hands, and carried away into the nearby woods.

Inside the fort area, the totally surprised British were massacred on every hand. Traders Bostwick and Solomon were among those within the enclosure, and they hurried to take refuge in garrets of the houses. As the Indians rushed into the fort, Bostwick says he saw a soldier, hotly pursued by an Indian, fleeing towards the open door of the house of a Canadian. The occupant of the house, M. Sans Chagarine, stood in the door watching the slaughter, and as the soldier drew near, the door was closed in his face. Whereupon the Indian promptly struck him in the head with his hatchet, and the soldier fell forward against the door with such force that he crashed it open.

Henry's Account of Massacre

Trader Henry was likewise among the British within the stockade, and his vivid story is the only detailed report of the massacre. "I did not go myself to see the match which was now to be played without the fort," he says, "because there being a canoe prepared to depart on the following day for Montreal, I employed myself in writing letters to my friends; and even when a fellow trader, Mr. Tracy, happened to call upon me, saying that another canoe had just arrived from Detroit, and proposing that I should go with him to the beach to inquire the news, it so happened that I still remained to finish my letters, promising to follow Mr. Tracy in the course of a few minutes. Mr. Tracy had not gone more than twenty paces from my door when I heard an Indian war cry and a noise of general confusion.

"Going instantly to my window I saw a crowd of Indians within the fort furiously cutting down and scalping every Englishman they found. In

"Going instantly to my window, I saw a crowd of Indians within the fort furiously cutting down and scalping every Englishman they found."—Alexander Henry.

particular I witnessed the fate of Lieutenant Jamet [the Officer of the Day]. I had in the room in which I was, a fowling piece, loaded with swan-shot. This I immediately seized and held it for a few minutes, waiting to hear the drum beat to arms. In this dreadful interval I saw several of my countrymen fall, and more than one struggling between the knees of an Indian, who, holding him in this manner, scalped him while yet living.

"At length, disappointed in the hope of seeing resistance made to the enemy, and sensible, of course, that no effort of my own unassisted arm could avail against four hundred Indians, I thought only of seeking shelter. Amid the slaughter which was raging I observed many of the Canadian inhabitants of the fort calmly looking on, neither opposing the Indians, nor suffering injury; and from this circumstance I conceived a hope of finding security in their houses. Between the yard of my own house and that of M. Langlade, my next neighbor, there was only a low fence, over which I easily climbed. At my entrance, I found the whole family at the windows, gazing at the scene of blood before them. I addressed myself immediately to M. Langlade, begging that he would put me into some place of safety until the heat of the affair should be over; an act of charity by which he might perhaps preserve me from the general massacre; but while I uttered my petition M. Langlade, who had looked for a moment at me, turned again to the window, shrugging his shoulders and intimating that he could do nothing for me: 'Que voudriez-vouz que j'en ferais?' [What do you want me to do?]

Henry Finds Refuge

"This was a moment for despair; but the next a Pani woman, a slave of M. Langlade's, beckoned me to follow her. [Indian slaves were frequently called "panis" because the earlier ones were captured from the Pawnee and kindred tribes in the far West—R. Mc.] She brought me to a door which she opened, desiring me to enter, and telling me that it led to the garret where I must go and conceal myself. I joyfully obeyed her directions; and she, having followed me up to the garret door, locked it after me and, with great presence of mind, took away the key. This shelter obtained, if shelter I could hope to find it, I was naturally anxious to know what might still be passing without. Through an aperture which afforded me a view of the area of the fort, I beheld, in shapes the foulest and most horrible, the ferocious triumphs of barbarian conquerors. The dead were scalped and mangled; the dying were writhing and shrieking under the unsatiated knife and tomahawk; and from the bodies of some, ripped open, their butchers were drinking the blood, scooped up in the hollow of joined hands and quaffed amid shouts of rage and victory. I was shaken not only with horror, but with fear. The suffering which I witnessed I seemed on the point of experiencing. No long time elapsed before every one being destroyed who could be found, there was a general cry of 'All is finished!' At the same instant I heard some of the Indians enter the house in which I was.

"The garret was separated from the room below only by a layer of single boards, at once the flooring of the one and the ceiling of the other. I could therefore hear everything that passed; and the Indians no sooner came in than they inquired whether or not any Englishmen were in the house. M. Langlade replied that he could not say—he did not know of any—answers in which he did not exceed the truth; for the Pani woman had not only hidden me by stealth, but kept my secret and her own. M. Langlade was therefore, as I presume, as far from a wish to destroy me as he was careless about saving me, when he added to these answers that they might examine for themselves, and would soon be satisfied as to the object of their question. Saying this, he brought them to the garret door.

Indian Search

"The state of my mind will be imagined. Arrived at the door, some delay was occasioned by the absence of the key, and a few moments were thus allowed me in which to look around for a hiding place. In one corner of the garret was a heap of those vessels of birch-bark used in maple sugar making. [It is quite probable that these vessels were *mokuks*, or Indian boxes, which were made by folding a piece of birch-bark—R. Mc.] The door was unlocked and opened, and the Indians ascended the stairs before I had completely crept into a small opening which presented itself at one end of the heap. An instant after four Indians entered the room, all armed with tomahawks, and all besmeared with blood upon every part of their bodies. The die appeared to be cast. I could scarcely breathe; but I thought that the throbbing of my heart occasioned a noise loud enough to betray me. The Indians walked in every direction about the garret, and one of them approached me so closely that at a particular moment, had he put forth his hand, he must have touched me. Still I remained undiscovered, a circumstance to which the dark color of my clothes and the want of light in a room which had no window, and in the corner in which I was, must have contributed. In a word, after taking several turns in the room, during which they told M. Langlade how many they had killed and how many scalps they had taken, they returned down stairs, and I with sensation not to be expressed, heard the door, which was the barrier between me and my fate, locked for the second time.

Henry Discovered

"There was a feather bed on the floor, and on this, exhausted as I was by the agitation of my mind, I threw myself down and fell asleep. In this state I remained till the dusk of the evening, when I was awakened by a second opening of the door. The person that now entered was M. Langlade's wife, who was much surprised at finding me, but advised me not to be uneasy, observing that the Indians had killed most of the English, but that she hoped I might myself escape. A shower of rain having begun to fall, she had come to stop a hole in the roof. On her going away, I begged her to send me a little water to drink, which she did. As night was now advancing I continued to lie on the bed, ruminating on my condition, but unable to discover a resource from which I could hope for life. A flight to Detroit had no probable chance of success. The distance from Michilimackinac was four hundred miles; I was without provisions; and the whole length of the road lay through Indian countries; countries of an enemy in arms, where the first man whom I should meet would kill me. To stay where I was threatened nearly the same issue. As before, fatigue of mind, and not tranquility, suspended my cares and procured me further sleep . . . .

Henry Delivered to Indians

"The respite which sleep afforded me during the night was put an end to by the return of morning. I was again on the rack of apprehension. At sunrise I heard the family stirring, and presently after, Indian voices informing M. Langlade they had not found my hapless self among the dead, and that they supposed me to be somewhere concealed. M. Langlade appeared, from what followed, to be by this time acquainted with the place of my retreat, of which no doubt he had been informed by his wife. The poor woman, as soon as the Indians mentioned me, declared to her husband in the French tongue that he should no longer keep me in his house, but deliver me up to my pursuers, giving as a reason for this measure that should the Indians discover his instrumentality in my concealment, they might revenge it on her children, and that it was better that I should die than they. M. Langlade resisted at first this sentence of his wife's; but soon suffered her to prevail, informing the Indians that he had been told I was in his house, that I had come there without his knowledge, and that he would put me into their hands. This was no sooner expressed than he began to ascend the stairs, the Indians following upon his heels.

"I now resigned myself to the fate with which I was menaced; and regarding every attempt at concealment as vain, I arose from the bed and presented myself full in view to the Indians who were entering the room. They were all in a state of intoxication, and entirely naked, except about the middle. One of them, named Wenniway, whom I had previously known, and who was upward of six feet in height, had his entire body covered with charcoal and grease, only that a white spot of two inches in diameter encircled either eye. This man, walking up to me, seized me with one hand by the collar of the coat, while in the other he held a large carving knife, as if to plunge it into my breast; his eyes, meanwhile, were fixed steadfastly on mine. At length, after some seconds of the most anxious suspense, he dropped his arm, saying, 'I won't kill you!' To this he added that he had been frequently engaged in wars against the English, and had brought away many scalps; that on a certain occasion he had lost a brother whose name was Musinigon, and that I should be called after him.

Henry's Life Spared

"A reprieve upon any terms placed me among the living, and gave me back the sustaining voice of hope; but Wenniway ordered me downstairs, and there informing me that I was to be taken to his cabin, where, and indeed everywhere else, the Indians were all mad with liquor, death again was threatened and not as possible only, but as certain. I mentioned my fears on this subject to M. Langlade, begging him to represent the danger to my master. M. Langlade in this instance did not withhold his compassion, and Wenniway immediately consented that I should remain where I was until he found another opportunity to take me away.

"Thus far secure I reascended my garret stairs in order to place myself the farthest possible out of the reach of insult from drunken Indians; but I had not remained there more than an hour, when I was called to the room below in which was an Indian who said that I must go with him out of the fort, Wenniway having sent him to fetch me. This man, as well as Wenniway himself, I had seen before. In the preceding year I had allowed him to take goods on credit, for which he was still in my debt; and some short time previous to the surprise of the fort he had said, upon my upbraiding him with want of honesty, that he would pay me before long. This speech now came fresh into my memory and led me to suspect that the fellow had formed a

Alexander Henry, English fur trader, explorer, author and survivor of the massacre of Fort Michilimackinac, in June, 1763. This drawing is based on a miniature painting; the autograph is from the Public Archives of Canada.

design against my life. I communicated the suspicion to M. Langlade; but he gave for answer that I was not now my own master, and must do as I was ordered.

A Hairbreadth Escape from Death

"The Indian on his part directed that before I left the house I should undress myself, declaring that my coat and shirt would become him better than they did me. His pleasure in this respect being complied with, no other alternative was left me than either to go out naked, or to put on the clothes of the Indian, which he freely gave me in exchange. His motive for thus stripping me of my own apparel was no other, as I afterward learned, than this, that it might not be stained with blood when he should kill me.

"I was now told to proceed; and my driver followed me close until I had passed the gate of the fort, when I turned towards the spot where I knew the Indians to be encamped. This, however, did not suit the purpose of my enemy, who seized me by the arm and drew me violently in the opposite direction to the distance of fifty yards above the fort. Here, finding that I was approaching the bushes and sand hills [remnants of these sand hills are visible today, behind the summer cottages—R. Mc.], I determined to proceed no farther, but told the Indian that I believed he meant to murder me, and that if so he might as well strike where I was as at any greater distance. He replied with coolness that my suspicions were just, and that he meant to pay me in this manner for my goods. At the same time he produced a knife and held me in a position to receive the intended blow. Both this and that which followed were necessarily the affair of a moment. By some effort, too sudden and too little dependent on thought to be explained or remembered, I was enabled to arrest his arm and give him a sudden push by which I turned him from me and released myself from his grasp. This was no sooner done than I ran towards the fort with all the swiftness in my power, the Indian following me, and I expecting every moment to feel his knife. I succeeded in my flight; and on entering the fort I saw Wenniway standing in the midst of the area, and to him I hastened for protection. Wenniway desired the Indian to desist; but the latter pursued me round him, making several strokes at me with his knife, and foaming at the mouth with rage at the repeated failure of his purpose. At length Wenniway drew near to M. Langlade's house; and, the door being open, I ran into it. The Indian followed me; but on my entering the house he voluntarily abandoned the pursuit."

Garret Again a Haven

Gaining the shelter of the house, Henry once more retired to his garret, strongly inclined, he says, to believe that, after being miraculously preserved so often, no Indian had the power to injure him. But about midnight his anxiety returned when the opening of the door startled him from sleep, and he was ordered to descend the stairs. He obeyed, and to his surprise and joy he found, in the room below, Captain Etherington, Lieutenant Leslie and trader Bostwick, together with Father Du Jaunay, the Jesuit missionary from L'Arbre Croche. The Indians were becoming intoxicated on the liquor they had seized, and to preserve their prisoners from being murdered during the debauch, the chiefs had permitted Charles de Langlade and the interpreter, Farly, upon giving their word of honor to return the captives when demanded, to take them to the fort under a guard of Indians. This provided the opportunity for Etherington, by the aid of Langlade, to send for the friendly Ottawa Indians and the missionary at L'Arbre Croche.

Henry's friends informed him that twenty Englishmen, including soldiers, were being held prisoners within the stockade, and he promptly joined the party in suggesting to Captain Etherington that an attempt be made to retake the fort from the Indians. The temptation to do this was strong. For the tribesmen had taken the fort during the attack, but in their eagerness to join in the drunken celebration, they had—with their usual slipshod method of waging war—failed to post a guard within the enclosure. So the Englishmen now planned to close the gates of the fort, and with the aid of the three hundred Canadian fur-trading employees, who were also inside the stockade, defend it against the Indians. Father Du Jaunay was consulted for his opinion of the scheme, but he advised against such an attempt; pointing out that the Canadians might prove unreliable and that failure of the undertaking would very likely result in the merciless slaughter of every remaining Englishman in the neighborhood. The idea was therefore abandoned, and Captain Etherington and his companions in misfortune spent the remainder of the night in Langlade's garret, comforting each other on their common lot.

The Canoe Journey

The next morning, the fourth of June, was cloudy and a cold northeast wind was sweeping in from Lake Huron. Only a small number of Indians were to be seen within the fort area, as most of them were now recovering from the effects of their victory spree. The scene of the previous days' bloody events was now dismal, forlorn and silent. A party of Indians, led by Wenniway, called for Henry and conducted him to a house inside the fort, leaving Captain Etherington, Lieutenant Leslie and trader Bostwick in the garret.

At this house, Henry was placed in a dark room where three other English prisoners were being held, and all now waited in suspense for the fate which lay before them. After a while, the four captives were led to a canoe drawn up on the wind-swept shore. Clad only in an old shirt (one of the Indians having, as will be recalled, forced him to give up his clothing in Langlade's house), Henry stood shivering on the beach, waiting to embark for an unknown destination. Charles de Langlade stood nearby watching the proceedings, and Henry asked him for a blanket, promising to pay him any price for it if he should live; but the Canadian—in strange contradiction to his many acts of kindness to the English during this critical time—refused to do so unless security was given for payment; observing that Henry's promise was now worthless since the Indians had robbed him of all the merchandise he owned in the country. However, another Canadian, John Cuchoise, proved more merciful and a blanket was provided which, Henry says, saved him from dying of exposure.

Captives Taken by Ottawa

The party, consisting of seven Indians and their four captives, now embarked in the canoe for Beaver Island, in northern Lake Michigan. One of the prisoners, a soldier, was tied to a crossbar of the vessel with a rope around his neck, in the customary Indian manner of transporting their captives; while the others were made to assist with the paddling. Their destination lay across the open lake, to the west, a course that ordinarily would have been taken; but a thick fog arose, and the Indians were compelled to keep close to shore for safety. In this manner they approached the lands of the Ottawa Indians, living on the eastern shore of Lake Michigan.

About every half hour, as they paddled along, the savages uttered a series of unearthly whoops,—one for each prisoner—a custom by means of which they informed anyone within hearing of the number of their captives. Several miles from the fort, when approaching Waugoshance Point,—across which the Indians carried their canoes to avoid going around it—they burst forth with this discordant signal. An Ottawa appeared on the beach in response and, calling to the party to land, he inquired the news and engaged the Ojibwa Indians, of the canoe, in conversation until they reached shallow water. Then suddenly a terrifying yell was heard—a hundred Ottawa Indians leaped out of the nearby woods—dashed into the water—seized the canoe and prisoners and hauled the Englishmen to shore. The Ojibwa, completely surprised by this action, protested in vain; while the captives now believed that their last sufferings were near at hand.

However, the course of the changing fortunes of the prisoners was not to end here. Instead of being led to their expected doom, they were greeted with a hearty hand-shake by Okinochumaki, the Ottawa chief, who assured them that they were among friends. They were told that they had been rescued from the Ojibwa, who, the Ottawa said, were carrying them to Beaver Island to be killed and devoured. But good will towards the captives really had little to do with this strange behavior of the Ottawa. For, as later became known, they felt insulted, and were angry because the attack upon the fort had been made without giving them a chance to share in the spoils and glory of so important a venture; and they took this means of giving vent to their disapproval.

Return to the Fort

The prisoners soon found themselves embarked in an Ottawa canoe, accompanied by a flotilla of Ottawa warriors, headed for Fort Michilimackinac; and towards evening they reached their destination. The Ojibwa at the fort were amazed to learn that their neighbors were taking sides against them; and they stood utterly dumbfounded as the well-armed Ottawa, with their captives, filed into the stockade and took possession of the stronghold.

The Englishmen were now lodged in the house of the commandant and closely guarded. So often overwhelmed with despair, their minds were now filled with hope that the Ottawa Indians would rescue them from their enemies who, as they had been told, intended to kill them to "make broth." But another reverse was still in store for the captives. On the following morning—June 5th—the Ojibwa invited the Ottawa to a general council within the fort. They brought a large present consisting of part of the plunder taken during the attack upon the fort, and they placed it in the center of the council chamber. Minavavana, the war-chief who had directed the outbreak, addressed the assembled Ottawa Indians.

Indians Divide Prisoners

He was greatly surprised, he declared, at their conduct in robbing them of their prisoners. He accused them of betraying the common cause of the Indians, and reminded them that all the tribes, with the exception of the Ottawa alone, had raised the hatchet against the English. Pontiac had taken Detroit, he told them; the King of France had "awakened from his sleep" and recaptured Quebec and Montreal; and the English were meeting with destruction, not only at Michilimackinac but throughout the entire world. (Minavavana very likely was given this incorrect information by a Canadian to encourage the Indians in their uprising.) He concluded by urging the Ottawa to abandon the cause of the English; to restore the prisoners and to take up the hatchet and join in the war.

The council adjourned until the next day; for, according to Indian custom, a reply was rarely given until the day after that on which arguments had been heard. Early the following morning the council was resumed and the Ottawa agreed to yield in part to Minavavana's request. They returned Henry and four of the soldiers to the Ojibwa, but retained Captain Etherington, Lieutenant Leslie, eleven soldiers and two traders—Solomon and Bostwick. These they carried to L'Arbre Croche where they treated them with kindness. In this manner the Ottawa and Ojibwa Indians adjusted their differences. However, the two tribes continued to regard each other with distrust; and it is said that the Ottawa never forgot the offense done them on the occasion of the massacre of Fort Michilimackinac.

The Ojibwa Prisoners

Henry and the four soldiers were now marched from the fort to the Ojibwa village near the shore, a short distance to the southeast. Here they were placed in a huge lodge, of the type that the Indians usually built in their villages for large public gatherings, such as dances, feasts and councils. Henry's soldier companions were bound together, and made fast to a support of the structure with a rope tied around their necks. The trader himself was left untied, free to find what comfort he could in a bed on the bare ground, with no other protection against the penetrating cold than an old shirt. For while they were saving his life, the Ottawa had robbed him of his blanket when they seized him, and the other prisoners, from the Ojibwa, on the shore of Waugoshance Point.

To add to the wretchedness of their perilous situation, the captives had had nothing to eat since the day of the attack upon the fort, four days before. Henry concedes that on the foggy morning in the canoe, the Ojibwa offered him and his comrades some bread—but bread, as he says, with what an accompaniment! The Indians sliced a loaf with the same knives they had used in slaughtering the victims of the massacre; knives that were still caked with dried blood. And moistening the blood with saliva, they rubbed it on the bread and, with fiendish glee, offered it to the Englishmen, telling them to eat the blood of their countrymen.

Henry Rescued by Wawatam

But distressing as was Henry's present lot, new cause for hope was in store for him. The morning after his return to the Ojibwa, the spacious lodge which served as the prison for him and his comrades, was filled with a gathering of Indians At the head of the enclosure was seated the war chief Minavavana, while beside him sat Wenniway, Henry's master who had adopted him and spared his life. Some of the Indians were giving vent to their hatred of the English by deriding and jeering at the captives, while the chieftains occupied themselves with discussing the fate they had in store for them.

Suddenly, Henry noticed an Indian stoop to pass through the low doorway of the lodge, and with a surge of joy, he beheld Wawatam, his adopted friend and brother, of whom he had heard nothing since the day before the massacre. As he passed, Wawatam shook the trader by the hand, advanced to the head of the lodge and sat down beside Wenniway and Minavavana. A short period of customary silent pipe-smoking followed and Wawatam arose and went outside, whispering to Henry as he passed, "Take courage." At length, he returned, followed by his squaw, both carrying an armful of presents which they laid before the assembled chiefs. Another period of silence ensued and Wawatam began to speak.

Wawatam's Appeal

"Friends and relations," he addressed the gathering, "what is it that I shall say? You know what I feel. You all have friends, and brothers, and children, whom as yourselves, you love; and you,—what would you experience, did you, like me, behold your dearest friend—your brother—in the condition of a slave; a slave exposed every moment to insult, and to the menaces of death? This case, as you all know, is mine. See there, [pointing to Henry] my friend and brother among slaves,—himself a slave!

"You all well know that, long before the war began, I adopted him as my brother. From that moment, he became one of my family, so that no change of circumstances could break the cord which fastened us together.

"He is my brother; and because I am your relation, he is therefore your relation too; and how, being your relation, can he be your slave? On the day on which the war began, you were fearful lest, on this very account, I should reveal your secret. You requested, therefore, that I would leave the fort and even cross the lake. I did so; but did it with reluctance. I did it with reluctance, notwithstanding that you Minavavana, who had command in this enterprise, gave me your promise that you would protect my friend, delivering him from all danger, and giving him safely to me.

"The performance of this promise I now claim. I come not with empty hands to ask it. You, Minavavana, best know whether or not, as it respects yourself, you have kept your word; but I bring these goods to buy off every claim which any man among you all may have on my brother as his prisoner."

The usual interval of silent pipe-smoking followed, for the Indians were very formal in their behavior in council. No bargain was made or important enterprise undertaken until the pipe had been puffed by all the parties interested, and the etiquette of the occasion had to be observed in every detail. This formality observed, Minavavana arose and replied:

Minavavana's Reply

"My relation and brother, what you have spoken is the truth. We were acquainted with the friendship which subsisted between yourself and the Englishman, in whose behalf you have now addressed us. We knew the danger of having our secret discovered, and the consequences which must follow; and you say truly that we requested you to leave the fort. This we did out of regard for you and your family; for if a discovery of our design had been made, you would have been blamed, whether guilty or not; and you would thus have been involved in difficulties from which you could not have extricated yourself.

"It is also true that I promised you to take care of your friend; and this promise I performed by desiring my son, at the moment of assault, to seek him out and bring him to my lodge. He went accordingly, but could not find him. The day after I sent him to Langlade's, when he was informed that your friend was safe; and had it not been that the Indians were then drinking the rum which had been found in the fort, he would have brought him home with him, according to my orders.

"I am very glad to find that your friend has escaped. We accept your present, and you may take him home with you."

Henry with Wawatam's Family

Wawatam thanked the chiefs and led Henry to his lodge, which stood within the Ojibwa village, only a few yards from the prison-lodge. Here the trader was received as one of the family. With true Indian hospitality,—for they were an extremely hospitable people—soft furs were spread for him to lie upon, and food in the usual generous quantities was immediately prepared for his first meal since the massacre, five days previously.

Slaughter of Prisoners

As he lay in Wawatam's lodge, the morning after his release, Henry was startled by a disturbance in the prison-lodge nearby. Peering through an opening in his shelter, he saw some Indians dragging out the dead bodies of the soldiers who had been his fellow prisoners. A noted chief, whom the Canadians called "Le Grand Sable" had just returned from his winter's hunt. He had arrived too late to take part in the attack upon the fort, and in his eagerness to display his hearty approval of what had been done, he had entered the prison-lodge and slaughtered the four prisoners with his knife. Had he arrived one day earlier, Henry might have been included among the victims.

The War-Feast

Under conditions of every-day life, the Indians were not cannibals. But after a victory it was customary for them to hold a formal war-feast—

a kind of religious rite—during which the bodies of their slain enemies were consumed, to increase —as they believed this would—their courage in battle, and to strengthen them to face death with fearlessness. Reasoning that like produces like, they felt certain that the virtues of the victims passed to those who consumed them; and that if they ate the body of a man who had been courageous, or a beast that was a good swimmer or a swift runner, then they would acquire some of these qualities or abilities themselves.

A feast of this nature followed shortly after the killing of the prisoners. Two of the Indians took one of the bodies, chosen as being the fattest, cut off the head and divided the remainder into five parts. These were placed in five kettles hung over separate fires at the door of the prison-lodge.

When everything had been prepared, a messenger came to Wawatam's lodge with an invitation to assist at the ceremony. Such invitations were given in the form of small cuttings of cedar wood, about four inches in length; and by word of mouth, the messenger delivering them, stated the particulars. For every important event in Indian life was done according to ritual, based on a rigid code of social customs. Wawatam responded to the invitation, on this occasion, by taking his wooden dish and spoon and going to the place where the kettles hung over the fires. After a while he returned, bringing in his dish a human hand and a large portion of human flesh. He did not appear to relish his gruesome repast, says Henry, and explained that he took part in the feast only to conform with this ancient custom of his people. For with all their wild notions of freedom and their impatience at all physical restraint, the Indians were so rigid in the observance of their ancient racial customs and traditions that they were often greater slaves to convention than white men living under the many restrictions of civilized society.

Capture of Trading Canoes

Towards evening, in the course of the day of the war-feast, a large trading canoe, occupied by several English traders, was seen out in the Straits approaching the fort from the east. A cry of warning arose from the Ojibwa village, and two hundred Indians raced to the landing place near the stockade. Apparently the canoe party had come from Montreal by way of the Ottawa River and Georgian Bay; and having heard nothing about the Indian uprising, they paddled confidently towards the fort. Suddenly, upon reaching shallow water, they were overwhelmed by the wild band of howling savages; dragged through the water, beaten, reviled, stripped of their clothing and thrown into the blood-spattered prison-lodge.

The Flight to Mackinac Island

About a week after the attack upon the fort, a change of feeling set in among the Indians. Up to this time all had been triumph and celebration; but now—like disobedient children—they began to fear the consequences of their behavior. Wild rumors were afloat that the English were coming to punish them for what they had done; and a growing uneasiness prevailed throughout the Ojibwa camp. A general council was held, at which it was decided to transfer the camp to Mackinac Island—a more defensible position in the event of an attack. So three hundred and fifty warriors and their families and household effects, and the prisoners taken from the trading canoe, now embarked on the voyage across the Straits. Wawatam and his family, in which Henry was included, accompanied the members of the savage flotilla. A gale arose during the crossing and the frail and heavily-loaded vessels pitched and tossed with such violence that the occupants began to fear they might be upset. Prayers were offered, and a dog with its legs tied was thrown into the lake as a sacrifice to calm the wrath of the offending manitou of the waters. The danger passed and the canoes approached the shores of the Island.

Suddenly, two squaws in the same canoe with Henry, burst forth with mournful cries of wailing and lamentation. With his thoughts still disturbed by recent experiences, and precarious as his position continued to be, the trader was very nervous and unusually sensitive to anything that threatened to give rise to more difficulties. These dismal sobs seemed to him like the forebodings of some new calamity, until he was informed that the squaws were merely observing the ancient custom of always displaying their grief when passing the graves of their relatives, who were buried on the nearby shore. (Perhaps these graves were in the old Indian cemetery which once occupied the site of the present Grand Hotel.)

The Camp on the Island

Arriving at the Island, the Indians began setting up their lodges; and before nightfall a savage community, with its many campfires and tall columns of rising smoke, had taken possession of the scene. Messengers from Pontiac drew their canoes up on the beach the following day, and urged the warriors of the village to go to his aid in the siege of the garrison at Detroit. But their taste for battle had been more than satisfied—at least for the present—and their sole concern now was to preserve themselves. Lookouts stood upon the cliffs during the day and a guard kept watch at night. In their jittery state the Indians spread frequent false alarms, and thus added to the anxiety of the much-agitated Henry.

Etherington Appeals for Help

Meanwhile, Captain Etherington and his companions had been carried to L'Arbre Croche. Here the commandant despatched two letters reporting the attack upon his post and entreating that aid be sent to him at once. One letter was carried by Father Du Jaunay to Detroit; but Major Gladwin and the small garrison there were still hotly besieged by Pontiac's warriors and very much in need of help themselves. On June 15, the other message was delivered by a party of Canadians and Ottawa Indians to Lieutenant James Gorrell, commandant of the fort at Green Bay, Wis., a post which was under the direction of the commandant at Michilimackinac. A copy of the message preserved in Gorrell's journal reads:

> Mishamakanak 11th June 1763
>
> Dear sir—
>
> The Second Instant this place was taken by surprize By the Chipways at which time Lieut. Jamet & Twenty more was kill'd & all the Rest taken prisoners but our Good friends the Ottaways have taken Lieutenant Lessley me & Eleven men out of their hands and have promis'd to Reinstate us Again. You'll therefore on the Receipt of this (which I send by a canoe of Ottaways) Sett out with all your Garrison and What English Trader you have with you and come with the Indian that Gives you this who will conduct you safe to me you Must be Sure to follow the Instructions you Receive from the Bearer of this as you are by no means Whatever to Come to this post before you See me at the Village Twenty Miles from this . . . I must once more beg you'll loose no time in Coming

to Join me and at the same time be very Careful and always be on your Guard I Long much to See you and am Dear Sir your Most humble Servant —

Geo. Etherington

J. Gorrell, Lieut.
Roy. Americans

Two years before, in 1761, when Michilimackinac was first garrisoned by the English, the post at Green Bay was taken over by Lieutenant Gorrell and his command of seventeen men. By a wise policy of friendship and generosity, he had succeeded in winning the good will and allaying the discontent of the nearby tribes of the Sauk, Fox, Menominee and Winnebago Indians. And this accomplishment, along with the fact that many of these tribesmen were not on good terms with the French, or the Ojibwa Indians of Michilimackinac, caused the Green Bay tribes to refuse to join in the general savage uprising. As a result, the British at Green Bay were left unmolested when the other posts were attacked.

Gorrell Goes to Rescue

When he received Etherington's call for help, Gorrell summoned the tribesmen to a council; told them of the attack made upon Michilimackinac by the Ojibwa, and explained that he and his men were going there to restore order. He distributed some presents, in the form of merchandise, among them and placed the fort in their care.

When he reached L'Arbre Croche, where Etherington and his fellow prisoners were held, Gorrell was warned that the Ottawa intended to disarm him and his men and to make them prisoners also; whereupon he gave notice that such an attempt would be vigorously resisted. However, contrary to this alarming report, the Ottawa received Gorrell and his men "with great joy, by the firing of several guns, three times each."

Several days of council holding followed, during which the friendly Green Bay Indians with Gorrell, induced the Ottawa to set the captives at liberty. However, an important obstacle stood in the way; for the Ojibwa Indians holding Fort Michilimackinac threatened to intercept the English if they should attempt to pass through the Straits on their way to Montreal. Another council was held. The Ojibwa, now in a state of alarm, and fearing an attack by the English, at length gave in, and consented to let the freed captives pass. So, on July 18, the party of Captain Etherington, Lieutenant Gorrell and their companions, consisting of forty canoes of soldiers, traders and Indian escorts, embarked from L'Arbre Croche, for Montreal, by way of Georgian Bay and the Ottawa River. They reached their destination safely on August 13; leaving not a single English soldier in the upper Great Lakes region except Major Gladwin and his command, who were busily engaged in the defense of Detroit.

Casualties of Attack Upon Michilimackinac

Of the unfortunate English garrison at Fort Michilimackinac, comprising the commandant, two officers and thirty-five men and the four fur traders, one officer (Lieutenant Jamet), twenty-four men and one trader (Tracy) were killed, while two men were wounded, as a result of the attack by the Indians. These latter two, along with nine other soldiers, Captain Etherington, Lieutenant Leslie and two traders, (Henry Bostwick and Ezekiel Solomon) had escaped to Montreal. Of the original body of Englishmen at Michilimackinac, Alexander Henry, the trader, was the only one who now remained in the region still alive.

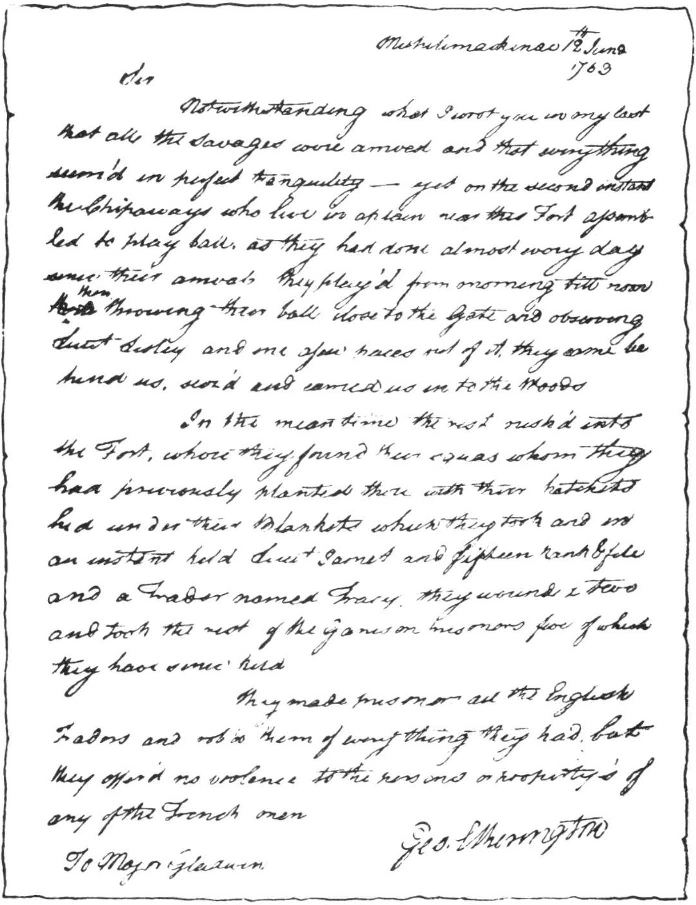

Michilimackinac 12th June
1763

Sir

Notwithstanding what I wrote you in my last that all the Savages were arrived and that every thing seem'd in perfect tranquility — yet on the second instant the Chipaways who live in a plain near this Fort assembled to play ball, as they had done almost every day since their arrival; they play'd from morning till noon then throwing their ball close to the Gate and observing Lieut Lesley and me a few paces out of it, they came behind us, seiz'd and carried us in to the Woods

In the mean time the rest rush'd into the Fort, where they found their squas whom they had previously planted there with their hatchets hid under their blankets which they took and in an instant kill'd Lieut Jamet and fifteen Rank & file and a trader named Tracy. they wounded two and took the rest of the Garrison prisoners five of which they have since kill'd

They made prisoners all the English Traders and robb'd them of every thing they had, but they offer'd no violence to the persons or property's of any of the French men

Geo. Etherington

To Major Gladwin

This is the first page of Captain Etherington's four-page letter to Major Gladwin, at Detroit, reporting the massacre at Fort Michilimackinac. Etherington's signature on this reproduction was taken from the third page of the letter. The original manuscript is in the Public Record Office, London, England.

And we shall now follow his fortunes after his rescue by Wawatam and his flight with the Indians to Mackinac Island.

Trading Canoes Captured

Several days after the Ojibwa moved to Mackinac Island, a prolonged cry of alarm was heard from the Indian encampment, and a large number of excited tribesmen were seen dashing towards the beach. The lookouts had caught sight of two large trading canoes coming up Lake Huron. So quickly manning their own canoes, the Indians paddled out into the Straits; and as the approaching vessels came around a point of shore, they swept down upon them and overwhelmed the terrified occupants. The trading canoes had come from Montreal by way of the Ottawa River with a cargo of trading goods for the fort, and the men in them apparently had heard nothing of the changed state of affairs at Michilimackinac.

Indian Drinking Bout

Among the booty found in the trading canoes was a large quantity of liquor; and as darkness fell, the discordant howls of drunken Indians arose from the village.

Although the distilling of intoxicating drink is common among savage people, somehow the idea never occurred to the Indians. And while rejecting the arts of civilization, something about their make-up caused them to take readily to one of the worst vices of white men—liquor, or "fire-water," as they called it. Yet, this would not necessarily have been tragic if the Indians had been able to drink moderately; but they saw no point in drinking liquor unless they could get intoxicated and bring on that joyful-new-world feeling of drunkenness. The result was the stuff

Major Henry Gladwin, British commandant at Detroit, in June, 1763, to whom Captain Etherington sent his message reporting the attack upon Fort Michilimackinac by the Indians. Although unable to send aid to Michilimackinac, Gladwin and his men saved their own post by withstanding the five-month siege of Pontiac and his warriors, thus preparing the way for the ruin of the Indian cause. This drawing is from an oil painting and the autograph is from the Clements Library.

ruined their health; and turned them into worthless drunkards, and madmen capable of the most devilish behavior.

Henry at Skull Cave

Realizing this latter feature, Wawatam knew that Henry's life would now be in danger—and desiring himself to take part in the spree—he quietly led the trader out of the camp, through the darkness, to a rocky cave on the high ground towards the interior of the Island. Making a bed of cedar boughs on the floor of the cavern, Henry wrapped himself in his blanket and slept soundly till daybreak. Upon awaking he felt a lump in his bed and, removing it, he found it to be a bone. At first he thought it had come from a deer, or a similar animal; but when full daylight arrived he discovered, with a feeling of horror, that he had slept through the night on a bed of human bones. When Wawatam failed to return at nightfall the trader moved his bed and spent the second night under a nearby bush, unable to meet darkness in the charnel-house, which made doubly gloomy his forlorn and perilous situation.

Indians at Skull Cave

At length, Wawatam appeared, full of apologies for the long absence caused by his alcoholic fling. Henry told him about the cave of bones, and upon examining it together they formed the impression that it had been filled, many years before, with human bones. Wawatam was unaware of its existence, in which he took a lively interest; and upon returning to the Indian village, he told his friends of the discovery. All expressed surprise and went immediately to see the cave; but after doing so they were as much puzzled as before, each offering a different opinion as to its history. Some thought that the bones were those of former inhabitants of the Island who had sought refuge in the cave, and were there massacred by the Huron (or Wyandot) Indians when this tribe fled westward, from their home on Georgian Bay, before the repeated assaults of the Iroquois. This event had occurred more than a hundred years earlier.

Others among the Indians suggested that the bones might be the remains of early inhabitants who had fled to the cave and were drowned there during the "great flood." For the traditions of the Ojibwa Indians tell of a deluge which resembles somewhat the deluge of the Bible. At the time of this disaster, according to one version, water covered the highest mountain of the earth, but not the top of a certain tree which grew on the summit of this mountain. By climbing this tree the Indian demi-god, Manabozho, saved himself, and stopped further rise of the waters. He then employed a muskrat to dive for a specimen of the original earth, and with this nucleus the world was rebuilt.

Indian Views of Nature

This is a typical Indian explanation of the operations of nature. Living in the midst of nature—and wise as they were in all the ways of nature—they were so poor at interpreting what they saw that they knew less than a modern school child about the laws of nature. Like other savage people—and some people among the so-called civilized races—they attributed to mysterious and supernatural causes happenings which can be explained on ordinary natural grounds. If the wind blew, it was because the wind lizard had crawled out of its pool. If the thunder was loud and frequent, it was because the young thunder birds were moving about in their nest; and if the corn crop was poor, the corn spirit was believed to be angry.

Struck with awe at the strange happenings surrounding them in nature, they regarded the sun, moon and stars, and every mountain, lake, stream and waterfall as manitous, or spirits, endowed with supernatural powers. And every bird, beast, tree, reptile, and even the smallest blade of grass, was believed to possess magical influence. However, with all their spirits, or gods, the idea of a single Almighty Being, the source of everything,—the Great Spirit—apparently did not occur to them until after their contact with white men. For the early Jesuit missionary, Father Claude Allouez, wrote that, "The savages of these regions recognize no sovereign master of Heaven and Earth, but believe there are many spirits." (The author once asked an Ottawa Indian, of good intelligence, what he thought the Indians said when they first saw the ships of Columbus. He replied that they probably exclaimed, "Manitous!" That is, spirits, or gods. From this it would seem that if a savage were to find a watch in the wilderness, instead of saying that it had been made by God—as William Paley, the English theologian, suggests that he would—it is probable that he would say the watch was itself a spirit, or god, like the ships of Columbus—not that it had been made by God.)

But however singular and varying their views might be on spiritual matters, the Indians were never known to kill anyone in a dispute about religious beliefs. Their sentiments in this regard were well summarized by one of their number who said that in affairs where men cannot agree, it is best to "let every man paddle his canoe on his own way." This tolerant attitude—and the general conduct of Indians before they became demoralized by contact with unscrupulous white traders and their liquor—indicate that the tribesmen had a better understanding of the Golden Rule than some white men who pride themselves on their Christianity and their presumed racial superiority.

Henry's Explanation of the Cave

Henry's explanation of the discovery in the cave is more plausible than that of the Indians. He believed that the cavern was the ancient receptacle for the remains of prisoners who had been devoured at war-feasts, such as the one he had witnessed only a few days previously. For he had observed that the Indians always gave special care to the bones of these ceremonies, preserving them unbroken in a place set aside for that purpose.

Today, this one-time Indian tomb, which trader Henry once used for a bed chamber in an hour of peril, is known as Skull Cave, one of the points of interest of Mackinac Island.

Henry in Indian Disguise

A few days after the incident at Skull Cave, the war chief, Minavavana, called at Wawatam's lodge and observed that many Indians were arriving daily who had taken part in the war around Detroit. Some of them had lost relatives in the fighting and the war-chief pointed out that they would very likely take vengeance on any Englishman they found. To guard against this danger, he thoughtfully suggested that Henry be disguised as an Indian; to which the trader readily consented, and the change was begun at once.

Henry's long hair—which was fashionable in those days—was shaved from his head, all except a spot on the crown about four inches in diameter. His face was painted with various colored clays and soot; and he was given a shirt colored with a mixture of grease and vermillion. A large collar of wampum, or Indian beads, was placed around his neck; silver bracelets on his arms, and his legs were covered with long hose of scarlet cloth, called *mitasses*. A gaudy blanket and a head-dress of feathers completed his make-up, which induced the squaws to remark that he made a good-looking Indian.

The Winter's Hunt

A shortage of food now struck the Indian camp and the inhabitants were often without anything to eat for days at a time. However, no words were wasted in useless complaint. Faces were blackened and "with a cheerfulness as if in the midst of plenty," all endured their hunger with that remarkable patience which is found among all Indians during times of unavoidable suffering and hardship. At length, the famine persisting, the tribesmen found it necessary to break camp and cross northward to the St. Martin Islands, where fish and wild fowl were found in abundance. Here Henry remained with Wawatam and his family until the approach of autumn, when the tribe dispersed and each family journeyed to its separate hunting-grounds. This was customary among the tribes of the region, because of the scarcity of game during the winter months.

Garbed in his Indian attire, Henry accompanied Wawatam and his family to the vicinity of the modern city of Ludington; where, amid the silence of the frozen forest, near where Father Marquette had died eighty-eight years before, he hunted bear, deer, beaver, raccoon, marten and otter. Commenting on this part of his adventures, when he found shelter from the winter's cold only in a frail Indian lodge, Henry says that he enjoyed more freedom than he had known for many years. "By degrees," he writes, "I became familiarized with this kind of life and had it not been for the idea of which I could not divest my mind, that I was living among savages, and for the whispers of a lingering hope that I should one day be released from it—or if I could have forgotten that I had ever been otherwise than I then was—I could have enjoyed as much happiness in this as in any other situation."

Attitude of Whites Towards Indian Life

Henry's favorable reaction towards the Indian mode of life is in agreement with the reports of many other white people who lived among the tribesmen for a while. In fact, there were many whites who, after having tried it, expressed a preference for the free but hazardous life of savagery to the more comfortable but restrained life of civilization. And large numbers of the whites—mostly young Frenchmen—actually abandoned civilized communities to go and live with the Indians. Some among the English settlers, who were taken prisoner in border raids,—particularly children who were captured and grew up among the Indians—declined an opportunity to return among their fellowmen.

Yet, while there were whites who preferred to live like the Indians, there were few, if any, Indians who regarded a completely civilized form of living as superior to their own way of life. This is true even of Indian children who were educated in the schools of white colonists and later permitted to return to their own people. With the opportunity of choosing between the two ways of life, they rarely cast their lot with civilization. This was because the Indians were convinced that the white man's style of life, with its lack of freedom; innumerable laws and taxes; extremes of wealth and poverty; snobbish class divisions; hypocritical customs; private ownership of lands; pent-up communities; uncomfortable clothing; manv diseases; slavery to money and other false standards, could not possibly bring as much real happiness as their own way of doing things.

Conflict Between Whites and Indians

However, while there were whites who favored the Indian mode of living, and a few bands of Indians whom optimistic whites thought were becoming civilized, the great mass of white people and the great mass of Indians realized that their two ways of life were directly opposed. Each race looked upon the other as inferior; neither felt inclined to adopt the ways of the other; and that is why the Indians and the whites could not get along together. A rapidly-growing community of civilized white men, depending on farming, manufacturing and trading—and forever reaching out for more lands—could not live in harmony with a race of hunters who needed wild lands for the preservation of the animals which provided them with their living.

One or the other of the two groups of people had to give up their accustomed mode of existence. And the longer the whites were in the country the plainer it became that the Indians, with their smaller numbers, lack of unity, inferior military equipment, and dependent—as they had become—on white traders for the needs of life, were a race of hunters and small farmers doomed to be strangers in their own country. Today, although deprived of most of their lands, and although many of their people have found it necessary to adopt the mode of life of white men, the Indians generally still prefer their own original way of living; and wherever possible they continue to preserve their ancient language, customs and beliefs, and to live, as much as they can, the free, unhurried, outdoor life of their ancestors.

Indian Conversation

The favorable attitude of the adult whites who liked Indian life is particularly remarkable, since trader Henry says that, for his part, he had to spend most of his leisure time smoking his pipe, due to the fact that he found the Indians very poor at conversation. "Among the Indians," he says, "the topics of conversation are but few, and limited, for the most part, to the transactions of the day, the number of animals which they have killed, and to those which have escaped their pursuit; and other incidents of the chase. Indeed the causes of taciturnity among the Indians may be easily understood if we consider how many occasions of speech which present themselves to us are utterly unknown to them; the records of history, the pursuits of science, the disquisitions of philosophy, the systems of politics, the business and amusements of the day, and the transactions of the four corners of the world."

Return to Fort Michilimackinac

With the appearance of the birds and blossoms of returning spring, Wawatam and Henry left their hunting-grounds and steered towards Fort Michilimackinac, which they reached April 27, 1764. Two French traders were now the sole inhabitants of the fort, and with these Henry bartered his furs for clothing, ammunition and tobacco. Wawatam erected his lodge near the lodges of other returning tribesmen, and eight days passed quietly when a band of Indians arrived from Saginaw Bay. These Indians were in quest of recruits for resuming the war around Detroit; and upon learning of Henry's presence they proposed to kill him, as they said, to bolster the courage of their comrades with a "mess of English broth."

Flight to the Sault

To escape such a fate Henry appealed to Wawatam to take him to Sault Ste. Marie, where the Indians, under the influence of Henry's friend, Jean Baptiste Cadotte, were known to be less hostile. Wawatam assented with his usual alacrity when Henry's life was in danger, and that night the party fled across the Straits to St. Ignace. Proceeding on their journey, an ill wind forced the travelers to put in at Goose Island, of "The Snows" group of islands, northeast of Mackinac Island. Here further progress was halted when Wawatam's squaw awoke complaining of a bad dream which she said foretold their destruction if the party continued on to the Sault. Familiar as he was with Indian customs and beliefs, Henry realized that dreams were regarded as a direct means of communication with the spirit world,—messengers which bore warnings from friendly manitous, whose indications must be observed to the letter if grave consequences were to be avoided. For this reason, everything to the tribesmen depended on their dreams; and as a result, their conduct was often as fickle as the weather. No labor or enterprise was undertaken contrary to indications from this source and whole war-parties were known to turn back if the dreams of a priest were unfavorable. Because of such beliefs as these the Indians, with all their physical freedom, lived in a veritable mental jail of tribal custom and superstition.

Aided by Friends to Sault

For Henry to have argued against the infallibility of dreams, on this occasion, would have made him appear not only disrespectful of Indian beliefs, but thoughtless as well of the safety of those who had done so much for him. So nothing was left but to resign himself to the disappointment, and to await the arrival of his enemies.

The island on which the party was encamped, lay along a main canoe route, and on the second day a canoe, bearing a sail, was seen approaching from the direction of Mackinac Island. Henry at first feared the worst; but his often-changing fortunes now turned again for the better, and instead of the enemy he feared, the vessel was found to be occupied by three Canadians and Madame Cadotte, the wife of Henry's friend at the Sault. Henry eagerly obtained permission to accompany the party to the Sault, and a round of heartfelt farewells were now exchanged with Wawatam and his family.

Wawatam's Farewell

Wawatam lit his pipe and presented it to the Englishman saying: "My son, this may be the last time that ever you and I shall smoke out of the same pipe! I am sorry to part with you. You know the affection which I always have borne you, and the dangers to which I have exposed myself and family to preserve you from your enemies; and I am happy to find that my efforts promise not to have been in vain." Wawatam and his family accompanied Henry to the beach, and as the canoemen plied their paddles away from the island, Wawatam stood praying aloud to the Great Spirit to take care of his brother until they should meet again.

At the Sault, Henry was heartily welcomed by M. Cadotte who sheltered him in a garret and induced his pursuing enemies to give up their designs on his life.

About a year had passed since Pontiac's followers had arisen against the English and the massacre occurred at Fort Michilimackinac. Efforts to restore peace among the faltering tribesmen were now being exerted; and a canoe bearing Indian messengers of peace arrived at the Sault from Fort Niagara, in New York. They had been sent out by Sir William Johnson, the English superintendent of Indian affairs, who was a man of remarkable understanding and wisdom in dealing with Indians. Like Frontenac, Duluth, Cadillac and others, he knew exactly when to use threats and when to make promises—both good tactics in the conduct of Indian relations. With his keen knowledge of Indian character, Johnson also knew that a policy of kindliness and moderation was to be resorted to only after he had employed firmness long enough to command the respect and obedience of the tribesmen. For, among the Indians, mildness was not expected in an enemy. They could see no point in waging war if prisoners were to be treated like long-lost brothers; and since they gave no quarter themselves, they expected none in return. Hence, if an enemy were to approach them in an attitude of gentleness and consideration, not knowing what to make of such strange tactics, they would interpret them as a sign of timidity and weakness. This would arouse their contempt, and produce a result the opposite of the one intended. So those skilled in handling Indians knew that the only way to make a favorable impression on the tribesmen was to talk to them with firmness and courage; for these were qualities which always commanded their respect and admiration.

Peace Message from Sir William Johnson

A council shortly ensued, at which one of the messengers, taking up a belt of wampum (used by the Indians in the place of written documents), made the following speech to the savage assemblage: "My friends and brothers, I am come with this belt, from our great father, Sir William Johnson. He desired me to come to you as his ambassador, and tell you that he is making a great feast at Fort Niagara; that his kettles are all ready, and his fires lit. He invites you to partake of the feast, in common with your friends, the Six Nations [the Iroquois tribes of New York], which have all made peace with the English. He advises you to seize this opportunity of doing the same, as you cannot otherwise fail of being destroyed; for the English are on the march with a great army, which will be joined by different nations of Indians. In a word, before the fall of the leaf they will be at Michilimackinac, and the Six Nations with them."

The Indians of the Sault had just been debating whether they should go to the aid of Pontiac at Detroit; but these words greatly disturbed them, and they responded by deciding to send a delegation of twenty representatives to Niagara. Alert to the possibilities that the decision offered for an escape, Henry eagerly sought, and obtained, permission to accompany the deputation on their voyage.

Invoking the Great Turtle

Arrangements for the departure were begun at once. But the project was too important to be undertaken without the aid of supernatural advice. So at nightfall, the Indian village, thronged with an excited concourse of warriors; old men and women; howling, flea-bitten dogs; and squaws with their numerous unruly children, was the scene of an elaborate and noisy ceremony. Hidden within a tent of moose-skins and attended by a horrible medley of yells, barks and howls, the nearly-naked Indian priest, or medicine-man, invoked the Great Turtle, the chief guardian spirit of the Ojibwa Indians.

Amid the din and violent shaking of the tent, a weak, shrill voice, like the whine of a puppy, was heard. This was immediately hailed by the savage assembly with a cry of joy, as the voice of the Great Turtle—the spirit who never lied. The village chief promptly greeted the spirit with a large offering of tobacco, for prayers and their answers were a kind of transaction in which the offering of tobacco (a sacred article among the Indians) was traded for the favor received. This item attended to, the chief inquired about the truth of the message conveyed by the envoys from Fort Niagara. The question was followed by more violent shaking of the tent—so violent that Henry expected to see it topple to the ground, although, in the darkness, he could not make out what was causing the disturbance.

A loud cry announced the departure of the spirit, and this was followed by a period of silence, during which, the Indians said, the spirit journeyed to Montreal. Upon returning, the spirit brought the alarming news that the St. Lawrence River was swarming with boats crowded with English soldiers, as numerous as the leaves of the trees, who were coming to make war on the Indians. In response to the chief's further inquiry, the spirit added that if the Indians visited Sir William Johnson at Niagara, they would be courteously received. Their canoes, they were told, would be filled with blankets, kettles, guns, powder, shot, and barrels of rum so huge that not even the strongest Indian could lift them; and everyone would return in safety to his family. This welcome information was received with loud expressions of joy; and clapping their hands in childish glee, a hundred savages declared their willingness to make the long journey.

Henry Consults the Great Turtle

The questions of public interest having been disposed of, the Great Turtle continued to be consulted by individuals of the Indian village regarding private matters, till nearly midnight. "Amid this general inquisitiveness," Henry says, "I yielded to the solicitations of my own anxiety for the future, and having first, like the rest, made my offering of tobacco, I inquired whether or not I should ever revisit my native country. The question being put by the priest, the tent shook as usual, after which I received this answer: That I should take courage and fear no danger, for that nothing would happen to hurt me; and that I should in the end reach my friends and country in safety. These assurances wrought so strongly on my gratitude that I presented an additional and extra offering of tobacco."

This ceremony of invoking the Great Turtle was common among the Great Lakes Indians, and their faith in the reliability of the answers given was unquestioning. As in the case of similar appeals for supernatural favors, one answer which turned out to be true worked like a prize won in a lottery —it was remembered while all the failures were forgotten. Henry says that although he made a special effort "to detect the particular contrivance by which the fraud was carried out," he was completely baffled by the violent shaking of the tent. This is quite understandable since the Indian priests were expert magicians and the ceremony took place in the dark of night. The early Jesuit missionaries were as much puzzled as Henry, by the strange behavior of the tent, and they said the whole business was the work of the devil. However, Samuel de Champlain, the Father of Canada, had witnessed the same ceremony among the Indians of Canada, and he says that he saw the priest, or medicine man, shake the supporting stakes of the tent.

Journey to Niagara

With all anxiety dispelled by the reassuring words of the Great Turtle, the Indian deputation, accompanied by trader Henry, embarked June 10, for the great peace pow-wow at Niagara. One day, during the journey, while in the vicinity of Georgian Bay, Henry was collecting firewood when his attention was attracted by an unusual sound which he thought came from above his head. Looking about him, he saw on the ground, only about two feet from his naked legs, a coiled rattlesnake, ready to strike. He hurried to his canoe to get his gun; but when, in answer to the inquiry of the Indians, he told them what he intended to do, they asked him to desist. With their pipes and tobacco-pouches in their hands, they followed him to the snake, and surrounding the reptile, they began addressing it as their "grandfather." They lighted their pipes and blew the smoke towards the snake, which appeared to Henry to receive it with real enjoyment.

"In a word," Henry says, "after remaining coiled and receiving incense for the space of half an hour, it stretched itself along the ground in visible good humor. Its length was between four and five feet. Having remained outstretched for some time, at last it moved slowly away, the

Indians following it and still addressing it by the title of grandfather, beseeching it to take care of their families during their absence, and to be pleased to open the heart of Sir William Johnson so that he might show them charity and fill their canoes with rum. One of the chiefs added a petition that the snake would take no notice of the insult which had been offered him by the Englishman, who would even have put him to death but for the interference of the Indians, to whom it was hoped he would impute no part of the offense."

Resuming their voyage, Henry and his Indian companions ran into a severe squall. Prayers and sacrifices were offered by the tribesmen to the god-rattlesnake; and one of the chiefs took a dog, tied its legs together, and threw it overboard; at the same time calling on the snake to preserve the party from drowning and asking it to satisfy its appetite with the carcass of the dog. Yet the wind blew. Another chief tossed a dog into the water, along with an extra offering consisting of tobacco. In his prayer accompanying the sacrifice, the Indian pleaded with the snake not to take vengeance upon him and his companions because of the insult that had been done the reptile by Henry in his intention to put it to death. He assured the snake that Henry was only an Englishman, and no relation whatever of the Indians. At the end of this prayer, an Indian sitting next to Henry in the canoe, remarked that if the party were drowned, it would be Henry's fault alone; and that he ought to be thrown overboard himself as a sacrifice to appease the angry manitou.

Arrival at Fort Niagara

Fortunately, however, before this extremity was deemed necessary, the storm at length abated; and a few days later, on the 22nd of June, the

Old Fort Niagara, N. Y., as it looks today. It was to this place that the British trader, Alexander Henry, and his Indian companions, made their canoe journey from S. S. Marie, in 1764, to attend Sir William Johnson's great Indian peace conference, following the Chief Pontiac War. Located thirteen miles from Niagara Falls, N. Y., ***at the point where the Niagara River empties into*** *Lake Ontario,* ***this historical*** *old fort, dating from 1725,* ***is*** *well maintained* ***and is open to visitors the entire year.***

party reached Fort Niagara, there to attend one of the largest gatherings of Indians ever held in North America. At Niagara, Henry was given a warm welcome by Sir William Johnson, who, aided by peace councils held by his deputy at Detroit, finally induced the Indians to give up their war against the English. In this way Henry's many harrowing experiences, which grew out of the attack upon Fort Michilimackinac, were brought to a close.

Return to Michilimackinac

Undaunted by these hardships and sufferings, Henry returned to the Great Lakes region two months later, with Colonel Bradstreet's force, sent to the relief of Detroit. Late in September, he arrived at Michilimackinac with Captain William Howard and his detachment of English and Canadians, who came to re-garrison Michilimackinac and other posts of the upper lakes. Henry managed to recover some of the goods that were taken from him during the massacre; and the following year he was granted a monopoly of the fur trade of Lake Superior. Later, he was engaged in an unsuccessful venture to mine copper in upper Michigan, and in exploring the Canadian Northwest. He was an associate of John Jacob Astor, and it is believed that Astor acquired much of his early knowledge of the fur trade under Henry's direction. Henry's closing years were spent at his home in Notre Dame St., Montreal. Before his death, at the age of eighty-five, he made three trips to Europe, during one of which he was presented at the court of the ill-fated Louis the Sixteenth and Marie Antoinette, the reigning royal family of France.

As for Captain Etherington, and the other survivors of the massacre, very little appears to be known about their future lives. Henry's surviving fellow traders, Ezekiel Solomon and Henry Bostwick, soon returned to continue their fur-trading pursuits in the Great Lakes region; and in 1768 they served as witnesses for Major Robert Rogers during his trial in Montreal. In 1781 Bostwick was a signer of the treaty by which Governor Patrick Sinclair purchased Mackinac Island from the Ojibwa Indians.

Wawatam's Memorial

Nothing is known about Wawatam, the Indian friend and benefactor of Henry, after their parting on Goose Island in May, 1764. Fifty years later, Henry Schoolcraft, while Indian Agent at Mackinac Island, sought vainly to find a trace of him and his family. His memory is preserved in the name of the giant railway car ferry which, for many years, has served, with the fidelity of its Indian namesake, as an important connecting link between the upper and lower peninsulas of Michigan.

Minavavana's Fate

Three years after the attack upon the garrison of the fort, the war-chief Minavavana was still at Michilimackinac, where he was encountered by Captain Jonathan Carver, a colonial army officer and explorer, under Major Robert Rogers, who tells of their meeting in these words: "The first I accosted were Chipeways, inhabiting the Ottawa lakes; who received me with great cordiality, and shook me by the hand, in token of friendship. At some little distance behind these stood a chief remarkably tall and well made, but of so stern an aspect that the most undaunted person could not behold him without feeling some degree of terror. He seemed to have passed the meridian

The** railway **ferry** "Chief Wawatam," operating between the upper and lower **peninsulas** of Michigan, **which is named after the** Ojibwa **Indian** who **rescued** the British trader, Alexander Henry, during the massacre of Fort Michilimackinac, in June, **1763.

of life, and by the mode in which he was painted and tattooed, I discovered that he was of high rank. However, I approached him in a courteous manner, and expected to have met with the same reception I had done from the others; but, to my great surprise, he withheld his hand, and looking fiercely at me, said, in the Chippewa tongue, 'Caswin nishishin saganosh,' that is, 'The English are no good.' As he had his tomahawk in his hand I expected that this laconic sentence would have been followed by a blow; to prevent which I drew a pistol from my belt, and, holding it in a careless position, passed close to him, to let him see I was not afraid of him . . . Since I came to England, I have been informed that the Grand Sautor, having rendered himself more and more disgustful to the English by his inveterate enmity towards them, was at length stabbed in his tent, as he encamped near Michilimackinac, by a trader."

End of Pontiac

With the failure of the French to lend the expected helping hand to the Indians, and the arrival of British reinforcements in the Great Lakes region, the back-bone of the Pontiac War was broken; and the Indians were in a mood to discuss peace. Pontiac, himself, fled westward, still bitterly hostile towards the English, although he had yielded to their offers of peace. At length, he was tomahawked by a hireling of a suspicious British trader, a member of the Illinois tribe, whose reward was a barrel of rum. "Whole tribes were rooted out to expiate the murder," writes the historian, Francis Parkman. "Chiefs and sachems, whose veins had thrilled with his eloquence, young warriors whose aspiring hearts had caught the inspiration of his greatness, mustered to revenge his fate, and from the north and east, their united bands descended on the villages of the Illinois . . . and the remnant of the Illinois who survived the carnage remained forever sunk in utter insignificance. Neither mound nor tablet marked the burial-place of Pontiac . . . and the race whom he hated with such burning rancor trample with unceasing footsteps over his forgotten grave."

Peace Restored

For more than a year after the English were driven from the Straits of Mackinac region, Fort Michilimackinac—which Captain Etherington had asked Charles de Langlade to look after—was frequented only by roving French traders and the Indians who came to trade with them. Late in September, 1764, Captain William Howard, of the 17th Regiment, arrived with a detachment of troops. He was given the keys to the fort gates by M. Pierre Parent, a Canadian who had relieved Charles de Langlade (now moved to Green Bay, Wis.), and Parent had "prevented the Indians from destroying the fort." Captain Howard called a council with the Ottawa and Ojibwa chiefs, and following the re-establishment of peaceful relations, the normal fur-trading life of the settlement was gradually resumed.

READING LIST

For those who feel a desire for more information about the subjects touched upon in these pages, the following books—obtainable at any modern public library—are recommended:

Historic Mackinac, by Edwin O. Wood.

Travels and Adventures, by Alexander Henry, edited by M. M. Quaife.

Conspiracy of Pontiac, by Francis Parkman.

Jesuits in North America, by Francis Parkman.

LaSalle and the Discovery of the Great West, by Francis Parkman.

French Regime in Wisconsin and the Northwest, by Louise P. Kellogg.

British Regime in Wisconsin and the Northwest, by Louise P. Kellogg.

First People of Michigan, by W. B. Hinsdale.

Michigan Historical Collection.

Wisconsin Historical Collection.

The Michigan Fur Trade, by Ida M. Johnson.

The Northwest Under Three Flags, by Charles Moore.

The Story of Michigan, by Claude Larzelere.

History of the Great American Fortunes, by Gustavus Myers.

Father Marquette, by Reuben G. Thwaites.

The Kingdom of Saint James, by M. M. Quaife.

The Voyageur, by Grace Lee Nute.

Astoria, by Washington Irving.

The Loon Feather, a novel by Iola Fuller.